# CONTENTS

# ACKNOWLEDGEMENTS

A glance at the Introduction or the Explanatory Notes will make clear the debt I owe to the late Wilmarth Sheldon Lewis, who edited *The Castle of Otranto* for this series. His life's work as a collector and disseminator of Walpoliana, and above all as the general editor of the Yale edition of *Walpole's Correspondence*, must inspire the gratitude and respect not only of all students of Walpole, but of those researching almost any aspect of eighteenth-century culture and society. I would also like to acknowledge Professor Joseph W. Reed's original annotation of *The Castle of Otranto* for Oxford University Press, which provided a basis for the critical apparatus of this revised edition.

E. J. C.

# THE CASTLE OF OTRANTO

HORACE WALPOLE (1717–97) was born in London, the youngest son of Sir Robert Walpole, and educated at Eton and King's College, Cambridge. Between 1739 and 1741 he toured France and Italy with the poet Thomas Gray. Soon after his return he became a Member of Parliament and in 1747 he bought the villa at Twickenham which he renamed Strawberry Hill. Remodelled, extended, and embellished in the 'gothick' style over two decades, it became a popular tourist attraction. He established a printing-press there and published many of his own works as well as those of others. Apart from *The Castle of Otranto* (1764) his books include the *Catalogue of Royal and Noble Authors of England* (1758) and *Historic Doubts on Richard III* (1768). He also left a vast collection of letters which, in the mingling of his wide interests, and in the wit, penetration, and inside knowledge they display, gives one of the finest pictures of life in eighteenth-century upper-class society, as well as a history of contemporary taste.

W. S. LEWIS was the lifetime editor of the Yale edition of *Horace Walpole's Correspondence* and author of a number of historical and biographical studies. He died in 1979.

E. J. CLERY is Professor of Eighteenth-Century Studies at the University of Southampton and author of *The Rise of Supernatural Fiction, 1762–1800* (1995).

## OXFORD WORLD'S CLASSICS

For over *100 years Oxford World's Classics have brought readers closer to the world's great literature. Now with over 700 titles—from the 4,000-year-old myths of Mesopotamia to the twentieth century's greatest novels—the series makes available lesser-known as well as celebrated writing.*

*The pocket-sized hardbacks of the early years contained introductions by Virginia Woolf, T. S. Eliot, Graham Greene, and other literary figures which enriched the experience of reading. Today the series is recognized for its fine scholarship and reliability in texts that span world literature, drama and poetry, religion, philosophy and politics. Each edition includes perceptive commentary and essential background information to meet the changing needs of readers.*

OXFORD WORLD'S CLASSICS

HORACE WALPOLE

# The Castle of Otranto
## A Gothic Story

*Edited by*
W. S. LEWIS

*With a new Introduction and Notes by*
E. J. CLERY

**OXFORD**
UNIVERSITY PRESS

# OXFORD
## UNIVERSITY PRESS

Great Clarendon Street, Oxford OX2 6DP

Oxford University Press is a department of the University of Oxford.
It furthers the University's objective of excellence in research, scholarship,
and education by publishing worldwide in

Oxford New York

Athens Auckland Bangkok Bogotá Buenos Aires Calcutta
Cape Town Chennai Dar es Salaam Delhi Florence Hong Kong Istanbul
Karachi Kuala Lumpur Madrid Melbourne Mexico City Mumbai
Nairobi Paris São Paulo Shanghai Singapore Taipei Tokyo Toronto Warsaw

with associated companies in Berlin Ibadan

Oxford is a registered trade mark of Oxford University Press
in the UK and in certain other countries

Published in the United States
by Oxford University Press Inc., New York

British Library Cataloguing in Publication Data

Data available

Library of Congress Cataloging in Publication Data
Walpole, Horace, 1717–1797.
The Castle of Otranto : a gothic story / Horace Walpole, edited
by W. S. Lewis.
(Oxford world's classics)
Includes bibliographical references.
I. Lewis, W. S. (Wilmarth Sheldon), 1895–1979.  II. Title.
III. Series.
PR3757.W2C3  1996  823'.6—dc20  96–4301

ISBN 978-0-19-953721-1

3

Printed in Great Britain by
Clays Ltd, St Ives plc

# INTRODUCTION

*The Castle of Otranto* originated in a dream; or so its author claimed:

I waked one morning in the beginning of last June from a dream, of which all I could recover was, that I had thought myself in an ancient castle (a very natural dream for a head filled like mine with Gothic story) and that on the uppermost bannister of a great staircase I saw a gigantic hand in armour. In the evening I sat down and began to write, without knowing in the least what I intended to say or relate. The work grew on my hands, and I grew fond of it—add that I was very glad to think of anything rather than politics—in short I was so engrossed in my tale, which I completed in less than two months, that one evening I wrote from the time I had drunk my tea, about six o'clock, till half an hour after one in the morning, when my hand and fingers were so weary, that I could not hold the pen to finish the sentence, but left Matilda and Isabella talking, in the middle of a paragraph.[1]

A 'very natural dream': for no man was better qualified to lose himself in a fantasy of the Middle Ages. The third son of the great Whig statesman Sir Robert Walpole, Horace Walpole was made financially independent by the bequest of a political sinecure. In 1747 he purchased a small villa in Twickenham on the outskirts of London, as a retreat from the hurly-burly of the capital, and over the next twenty-five years proceeded to transform it into a gothic[2] castle in miniature, filled with art objects, curios, and rare books. Others before him had toyed with decorative garden ruins or pinnacled fireplaces, but never had the Gothic style in

[1] The Yale edition of *Horace Walpole's Correspondence*, ed. W. S. Lewis *et al.*, 48 vols. (New Haven, 1937–83), hereafter referred to as *Walpole's Correspondence*; 1. 88 (letter to William Cole, 9 Mar. 1765).

[2] I have used 'gothic' with an initial lower case to refer to the historical period; 'Gothic' with an initial capital refers to the 18th-c. aesthetic movement.

architecture been so thoroughly or passionately revived as at Strawberry Hill. In planning the alterations, Walpole pored over ancient folios, took notes on the genuinely gothic cathedrals and castles visited on summer tours, and set up a 'Committee of Taste' consisting of himself and two antiquarian friends to deliberate over every detail. But at the same time he freely admitted the artificiality of the enterprise: his inner vision was realized with wood, plaster, and *trompe-l'œil* wallpaper.

It was in the pleasing 'gloomth' of Strawberry Hill that Walpole fell asleep on that night early in June 1764 and had a nightmare; and it was there, surrounded by old tomes and suits of armour, the light filtering through stained-glass windows, that he began to write *The Castle of Otranto*. The novel has often been described as a spontaneous, almost unconscious, extension of the dilettante's activities. This idea, along with the bizarre, dream-like quality of the narrative itself, led André Breton and the French Surrealists to claim Walpole as one of their own. Paul Éluard, in his introduction to a 1943 translation of *Otranto*, paid the ultimate compliment of comparing the opening scene of the novel to a famously surreal image from Lautréamont's *Les Chants de Maldoror*: with the incident of Conrad '"dashed to pieces, and almost buried under an enormous helmet, an hundred times more large than any casque ever made for human being, and shaded with a proportionable quantity of black feathers", we already have the chance encounter on a dissecting table of a sewing machine and an umbrella'.[3] There have also been attempts to apply Freud's methods and analyse *Otranto* as a dream rather than as a work of literature—an exercise which predictably enough has revealed a welter of incestuous and parricidal desires behind the smooth façade of the eighteenth-century man of letters.[4]

---

[3] Cit. Maurice Levy, *Le Roman 'Gothique' anglais 1764–1824* (Toulouse, 1968), 109; my trans.

[4] See Harfst and Kallich in the Select Bibliography.

And yet, the dream-origin of *The Castle of Otranto* has been mentioned more often as an explanation for its short-comings, than as a cause for enthusiasm. From the start, its wildness invited derision. One friend of Walpole, Gilly Williams, wrote to another, George Selwyn, complaining of *Otranto*'s tedious outlandishness: 'He says it was a dream, and I fancy one when he had some feverish disposition in him.'[5] Walpole himself was sometimes inclined to dismiss it as a piece of whimsy, and in the twentieth century critics have tended to agree. The story has been regularly censured for wooden characterization, and the amateurish self-indulgence of its supernatural effects.

It may seem strange that a work which has received a good deal of negative criticism nevertheless continues to attract so much attention, and indeed, after close to a hundred editions in many languages, continues to be reprinted in paperback form today. The main reason, both for the criticism and for the resilience of this work, is surely that *The Castle of Otranto* is never judged purely on its own merits, but rather as the founding text of a genre that has flourished, through various permutations, up to the present. Walpole never wrote another novel, but his example was followed by others in increasing numbers until by the 1790s an identifiable mode of 'modern romance' or 'terrorist fiction' was taking the book market by storm. In the course of the nineteenth and twentieth centuries, 'Gothic' has diversified into many sub-genres, including historical romance, science fiction, and detective fiction. The slender tale of *Otranto* might well appear as insubstantial as poor Conrad beneath the weight of such a legacy. That it is still read, and read with interest, is something of a tribute to Walpole's foresight, as well as to his imaginative powers.

Walpole was the first to propose establishing a modern 'Gothic' style of fiction, and it was a proposal that at the

---

[5] *Walpole's Correspondence*, 30. 177 (19 Mar. 1765).

time required considerable audacity. For when he introduced the subtitle 'A Gothic Story' in the second edition of
*Otranto*, he was overturning some cherished assumptions.
The precise nature of this challenge to orthodoxy will require a little untangling, in order to avoid a simplistic for-
mula of revolutionary romanticism versus neoclassical
stagnation. For much of the century, 'gothic' was a term
used synonymously for 'uncouth' or 'barbaric' when refer-
ring to art or manners. Artefacts of the Middle Ages, because of their extravagance and irregularity, fell foul of the
established standards of aesthetic propriety. But by the
1750s there was a new interest in the gothic inheritance.
This applied first to architecture, and was extended to literature by two important works of criticism, *Observations on
the Faerie Queene of Spenser* (1754) by Thomas Warton and
*Letters on Chivalry and Romance* (1762) by Richard Hurd,
both arguing that gothic writing should be appreciated on
its own terms, as the product of other times.

Hurd was also among those who suggested that the
gothic age, precisely because of its relative barbarity, was
especially conducive to the free play of imagination, and
that what the modern era had gained in civility it had lost in
poetic inspiration. The currency of this notion does something to explain the curious manner of appearance of one of
the great publishing successes of the century, the Ossian
epics, *Fingal* (1762) and *Temora* (1763). These poems were
presented to the public as the work of a Gaelic Bard of the
fourth century AD, but were actually concocted by James
Macpherson, intent on providing Britain with a rival to
Homer. There was debate over their antiquity, but most
admirers, until well into the next century, preferred to take
them as irrefutable evidence of gothic genius. (Walpole was
an exception; while he appreciated the poems, he was convinced they were fake.) Issues of Scottish nationalism were
an important factor in the 'Ossian' phenomenon, but the
fraud itself was in large part the product of two conflicting

pressures: on the one hand a growing enthusiasm for the superstitious fancies of the past; and on the other, a sense that this kind of imaginative freedom was forbidden, or simply impossible, for writers of the enlightened present.

The same pressures doubtless played a part in Walpole's decision to present *The Castle of Otranto* to the public in the guise of an ancient manuscript, recently discovered. In the Preface to the first edition, which was published on Christmas Eve 1764, he assumes the persona of a translator, 'William Marshall, Gent.', and offers learned speculations about the date of the text, the Italian in which it was originally written, and the author's propagandist aims, as well as some cheeky words of praise for the 'beauties' of his 'adopted work'. To his delight, many readers took the bait, including a reviewer in one of the most prestigious periodicals of the day, the *Monthly Review*. His friend the Revd William Mason later wrote to assure Walpole that he himself had been entirely duped: 'When a friend of mine to whom I had recommended *The Castle of Otranto* returned it me with some doubts of its originality, I laughed him to scorn, and wondered he could be so absurd as to think that anybody nowadays had imagination enough to invent such a story.'[6] But rather than maintaining the pretence, as Macpherson did with 'Ossian', success encouraged Walpole to publish a second edition in April 1765, with a new Preface confessing his authorship.

The significance of *Otranto* for literary history lies as much in the two Prefaces and their alternative constructions of the text as antiquity or innovation, as it does in the novel itself. Readers of the first edition had been led to believe that it was written by a scheming priest, bent on encouraging superstition 'in the darkest ages of christianity'; now, with the initials 'H.W.' added to the second edition, it was discovered to be the work of a living Member of Parliament

[6] *Walpole's Correspondence*, 28. 5 (14 Apr. 1765).

and prominent figure in fashionable society. Walpole could have passed the ruse off as a joke, but instead he chose to make the second Preface a manifesto for a new kind of writing, a 'blend' of the 'imagination and improbability' found in ancient romance, and the accurate imitation of nature that is the hallmark of the modern novel. *Otranto*, having been a dream and a counterfeit, was now reconstructed as a 'new route' for 'men of brighter talent to follow'.

Modern authors had, in fact, already been experimenting with some of the romance elements to be found in *Otranto*. As early as 1706 Daniel Defoe, better known for his realist novels, had written a ghost story, *A True Relation of the Apparition of One Mrs Veal*. It became a familiar item in literary anthologies; yet the flat, journalistic style reveals its true purpose: to confront doubters with documentary evidence of the immortality of the soul—an aim shared by other religious writers, particularly Dissenters. Most good Anglicans, however, eschewed belief in ghosts as popish nonsense. Edward Young in *Night Thoughts* (1742–5) and Robert Blair in *The Grave* (1743) used macabre imagery, without any actual apparitions, to enhance serious reflection on mortality, and in doing so launched the 'Graveyard School' of poets. Tobias Smollett introduced a similar mood of supernatural terror into popular fiction in some scenes from *Ferdinand Count Fathom* (1753), but here it was subordinate to satire of contemporary society. Conversely, Thomas Leland's *Longsword* (1762) was set in the gothic past, but without any hint of the marvellous or the morbid.

The writers who came closest to defying contemporary expectations, prior to *The Castle of Otranto*, were probably William Collins and Walpole's close friend Thomas Gray, in a number of odes dealing with fear and superstition. Gray's 'The Bard: A Pindaric Ode' was first published in 1757 at Walpole's private Strawberry Hill Press, and in-

volves, like *Otranto*, a tyrant, a prophecy, and ghosts demanding vengeance. The poem met with a frosty reception
from the critics, and the notorious difficulty of Gray's system of allusion stood in the way of wider appreciation. This
failure, illustrating the conservatism of the literary establishment, may well have been in Walpole's mind when he
wrote his polemical second Preface.[7] His 'Gothic Story' had
proved a success in its antiquarian disguise, and he could
afford to annoy the critics. Making a pre-emptive strike at
the prevailing mode of realist fiction, he declares: 'The great
resources of fancy have been dammed up, by a strict adherence to common life.' He seems to have had in mind chiefly
the example of Samuel Richardson, author of *Pamela* and
*Clarissa*; in a letter to Elie de Beaumont he explains that he
is sated with run-of-the-mill sentimental novel-writing and
finds Richardson's realist fictions 'insupportable'. His own
creation would serve as an antidote: 'a god, at least a ghost,
was absolutely necessary to frighten us out of too much
senses [*sic*].'[8]

Two years later Walpole was still revelling in the pose of
the inspired subversive: 'of all my works, it is the only one
which has pleased me; I gave rein to my imagination; visions
and passions heated me. I did it in spite of rules, critics, and
philosophers.'[9] But although the novelty of *Otranto* is un-
deniable, the rhetoric of originality Walpole employs be-
longs to a strand in literary criticism which had long formed
a counterpoint to neo-classical insistence on decorum.
Joseph Addison, for instance, had written with some enthusiasm about fantasy literature in his essays on *The Pleasures
of the Imagination* (1712). While admitting that success in
this mode depended on a 'very odd turn of Thought' and

[7] It is interesting to note Walpole's remark that originally *Otranto* 'met
with too much honour by far, for at last it was universally believed to be
Mr. Gray's'; *Walpole's Correspondence*, 38. 525–6 (letter to Hertford, 26
Mar. 1765).

[8] Ibid. 38. 379 (18 Mar. 1765).

[9] Ibid. 3. 260 (to Mme Du Deffand, 13 Mar. 1767).

'an Imagination naturally fruitful and superstitious', and that such writing could not appeal to everyone, Addison nevertheless gave it the credit of Englishness ('the *English* are naturally Fanciful'), and presented Shakespeare as the great exemplar.[10] Over the next half-century, more elaborate justifications for rule-breaking were developed, above all the ideas of original genius and the sublime. Edward Young in *Conjectures on Original Composition* (1759) contrasted the divine ability of genius to inspire and elevate, with the mundane achievements of the 'meddling ape, *Imitation*'. Edmund Burke's *A Philosophical Enquiry into the Origin of our Ideas of the Sublime and the Beautiful* (1757) was immediately influential, and favourably contrasted the powerful sublime, illustrated by passages from Homer, Shakespeare, and Milton, with the merely beautiful, linked with social pleasures and imitation.

In every case, Shakespeare emerged as that paradoxical thing, the model of 'untutored genius', the pattern of originality. Walpole was by no means unique in submitting his plea for imaginative liberty under shelter of the Immortal Bard; his second Preface is a notable contribution to the emerging cult of Shakespeare. There, he pursues a fairly standard strategy of identifying the constraints of neo-classical criticism with France; but the assault on Voltaire was the most thoroughgoing that had yet appeared. The great *philosophe* had had the temerity to find fault with the unorthodox dramatic practice of Shakespeare, while applauding the correct but bland productions of his countrymen. Accordingly, Walpole's fanciful tale takes on the appearance of a nationalist enterprise; and breaking the rules of literary decorum by including a few phantoms, or mixing comedy and tragedy, becomes almost a patriotic duty. Although *The Castle of Otranto* was published in the year following the conclusion of the Seven Years War

[10] D. F. Bond (ed.), *The Spectator*, 5 vols. (Oxford, 1965), No. 419, 'Fantasy: writing wholly out of the poet's own invention', pp. 570, 572.

against France, it is clear that hostilities on the aesthetic front had not yet ceased.

There are many echoes of Shakespeare in *Otranto*, but although certain scenes and devices may be derivative, this does not undermine the novel's central claim to innovation. For whereas previous defences of gothic writing and 'irregular' imagination had served to increase appreciation of works by authors of the past, such as Spenser and Shakespeare, Walpole's idea was to write using the same devices in the present, but in a style adjusted to contemporary tastes. Hence the resonance of the new subtitle to the second edition: it was at precisely the moment that *Otranto* was revealed to be a modern work that the adjective 'gothic' was first applied to it. There is a dislocation: 'Gothic' is no longer a historical description; it marks the initiation of a new genre.

For the reader of today, coming to *Otranto* after more than two centuries of Gothic writing, many of its elements will appear instantly, if not uncannily, familiar. To begin with there is the castle which dominates the narrative as both a physical and a psychological presence, and rightly assumes its place in the title. Few critics have failed to make the point that the gothic castle is the main protagonist of the *Otranto*, and that the story of usurpation, tyranny, and imprisonment could be seen as an extension of the mood evoked by the setting. All of the action takes place either in or near the castle, and its layout is described with precision. But more important than physical immediacy is the atmosphere of oppression created by the place, and the way it emphasizes the powerlessness of the characters, manipulated by forces they only dimly comprehend. Architecture becomes the embodiment of fate, and it is entirely in keeping that it should feature so dramatically in the grand finale.

The effect of the story as a whole depends on vivid, static images, rather than a gradual build-up of suspense.

Fragmentation is the order of the day, and the stage properties are vital. The prominence of 'claptrap' has been seen as a flaw, but it undoubtably had a powerful impact on readers of the time. One of the earliest imitations of *Otranto*, 'Sir Bertrand. A Fragment', which appeared in *Miscellaneous Laetitia Writings* (1773) by John and Anna Letitia Aikin, abandons narrative coherence altogether in favour of a kaleidoscopic succession of Gothic effects: a knight on horseback, a ruined mansion, a blue flame, a shriek, and a disembodied hand on a banister (in homage to Walpole's original dream-image); after which the text breaks off abruptly. One scene from *Otranto* especially captured the imaginations of contemporaries, thanks to setting and props. Isabella desperately fleeing through a subterranean passage by candlelight was the image that launched a thousand similar flights. Blake responded with 'Fair Eleanor', a poem in which the heroine is glimpsed,

> like a ghost, thro' narrow passages
> Walking, feeling the cold walls with her hands.
>
> (ll. 11–12)

Jane Austen in turn offered her tribute to the candle that blows out at the crucial moment, in her affectionate parody of the Gothic mode, *Northanger Abbey* (1818). Indeed, satires of Gothic, which begin to appear from the 1790s, are a good indication of the relative importance of *things* (as distinct from character, plot, or dialogue). They were often presented in the form of 'recipes':

> *Take*—An old castle, half of it ruinous.
> A long gallery, with a great many doors, some secret ones.
> Three murdered bodies, quite fresh.
> As many skeletons, in chests and presses.
> An old woman hanging by the neck; with her throat cut.

Assassins and desperadoes, '*quant. suff.*'
Noise, whispers, and groans, threescore at least.
Mix them together, in the form of three volumes, to be taken at any
of the watering places before going to bed.[11]

The generic importance of the castle of Otranto and its
contents is well established, but there has been some dissent
over Walpole's treatment of the inhabitants. In the first
Preface, in the role of translator, Walpole took it upon
himself to praise the delineation of the characters, and was
promptly echoed by a reviewer: 'the characters are highly
finished; and the disquisitions into human manners, passions, and pursuits, indicate the keenest penetration, and the
most perfect knowledge of mankind'.[12] Both, it should be
remembered, were judging the text as if it were a medieval
manuscript. In the second Preface, there is a more modest
proposal that the characters have been made to 'think, speak
and act, as it might be supposed mere men and women
would do in extraordinary positions'. In twentieth-century
criticism, some enthusiasts have suggested that *Otranto* ini-
tiates a turn towards the exploration of new psychological
depths. The claim has been countered by the accusation that
eighteenth-century writers of Gothic in general, and
Walpole in particular, are guilty of peopling their stories
with mere ciphers.[13] The perceived failure has sometimes
been attributed to a lack of ability in the authors, sometimes
interpreted as a symptom of the troubled times in which the
novels were written. But in the most recent critical discussion, the problem of whether or not Gothic fiction achieves
depth of characterization has been displaced by a new interest in surfaces.[14] The rhetorical gestures, the moulding of

[11] 'Terrorist Novel Writing', in *The Spirit of the Public Journals for 1797*
(London, 1798), 223–5.
[12] *Monthly Review*, 32 (Feb. 1765), 97–9.
[13] See Kiely and Napier in the Select Bibliography.
[14] See Henderson, Hogle, and Sedgwick in the Select Bibliography.

physiognomy into hieroglyphs of rage or despair, the mysterious interchangeability of individuals suggested by frequent instances of mistaken identity, are all, according to this alternative account, signs of a Gothic code of selfhood at odds with the 'three-dimensional' characters of realist fiction. In Gothic, the argument goes, identity is not determined from the inside out, but from the outside in; it is a matter of public interpretation rather than private expression, and to this extent the horror mode tells an important truth about the role of social convention in constituting subjectivity—one which 'common sense' would tend to deny.

At first glance, the novel seems to offer the basic stock of Gothic character-types, but closer attention suggests an ambivalence in each of them that verges on irony. There are two virtuous young ladies in distress, one of whom, Matilda, possesses the quintessential Gothic name. But the gravity of their plight is strangely undermined by a spat over their mutual love-object, Theodore. Theodore himself is a bland young hero; his role as a disinherited nobleman raised as a peasant was already a standard feature of romance, and would be used again in Clara Reeve's *The Old English Baron* (1777), while Ann Radcliffe adopted the name for the hero of *The Romance of the Forest* (1791). But whereas Radcliffe's Theodore succeeds in rescuing the heroine, at least temporarily, from the hands of the villain, the only act of valour Walpole's Theodore performs is blunderingly to wound the father of Isabella. A sense of disappointment or bathos equally hangs over the rest of the cast. Father Jerome and Frederic, Count of Vicenza, introduced as staunch opponents of the tyrant Manfred, soon show signs of weakness that will contribute to the tragic outcome. Hippolita is the prototype of a long series of victimized wives, most notably, in the period, the wretched prisoners of Radcliffe's *A Sicilian Romance* (1790) and Regina Maria Roche's *The Children of the Abbey* (1796). But her situation is never so affecting as theirs; she wanders freely if pathetically through the castle, her passivity a positive aid to Manfred's villainy.

'Manfred, prince of Otranto': these are the opening words of the novel, and Manfred is of all the characters the most developed. Only he fully appreciates the import of the prophecy that hangs over his family, and the plot is propelled by his frantic attempts to circumvent the inevitable outcome. Manfred's temperament, naturally humane we are told, has been brutalized by his fate; he is a draft version of the fascinating anti-hero which Byron would later perfect. But no Byronic hero ever had to deal with the degree of aggravation that Manfred endures. He is blocked at every turn not only by supernatural phenomena, but even more effectively by his own servants, whose panics, long-winded explanations, and compromising *faux pas* drive him into paroxysms of helpless fury. Walpole set great store by his inclusion of the servants as a light-hearted contrast to the central drama, and was no doubt delighted by the judgement of his friend Cole that Matilda's maidservant, Bianca, was 'very Nature itself',[15] and by the indirect compliment paid by Radcliffe and Lewis when they imitated the device. Shakespeare is the precedent, but Elizabeth Napier is surely right in suggesting that whereas the humour of the Porter in *Macbeth* or of the Gravediggers in *Hamlet* augments the serious concerns of the plays, the servants in *Otranto* tend merely to undermine the woes of their masters, repeatedly bringing about a comic deflation. Manfred does his best as a tyrant in the mould of Macbeth, but his gravity suffers terribly at their hands. In Charlotte Brontë's *Shirley*, Ann Radcliffe's *The Italian* is described as ending 'in disappointment, vanity and vexation of spirit'. The judgement applies more truly to the conclusion of its Gothic precursor, *The Castle of Otranto*.

[15] *Walpole's Correspondence*, 1. 91–2 (17 Mar. 1765).

The plot is an aspect of the novel for which Walpole has often been praised; it is, as he boasts in the first Preface, fast-paced and streamlined: 'Every thing tends directly to the catastrophe.' There is a quality at once relentless and strangely haphazard about the chain of events, triggered by a cause which is partially concealed. As Robert Kiely remarks, 'the plot is part obstacle course, part free-for-all, and part relay race in which the participants run through a cluttered labyrinth passing the baton to whomever they happen to meet'.[16] It is the reverse of Radcliffe's leisurely, topographical adventures, but an obvious forerunner of sensationalist fictions like *The Monk* (1796) by M. G. Lewis, *Horrid Mysteries* (1796) by Karl Grosse, and Percy Shelley's two excursions into the terror mode, *Zastrozzi* (1810) and *St Irvyne* (1811). Despite the use of some devices of deferral—interrupted revelations, abrupt scene-shifting, mistaken identity, the garrulous servants—Walpole's purpose is to overwhelm the reader with an excess of stimuli, rather than to tantalize.

The nature of the plot may be uncontroversial, but this has not prevented disagreement over the response it is intended to produce: terror, pity, or even laughter? In the first Preface, Walpole invokes Aristotle's theory of catharsis in tragedy, from the *Poetics*: 'Terror, the author's principal engine, prevents the story from ever languishing; and it is so often contrasted by pity, that the mind is kept up in a constant vicissitude of interesting passions.' When William Warburton praised the novel, it was along the same lines: 'a beautiful imagination, supported by strength of judgment, has enabled the author to go beyond his subject and effect the full purpose of the *ancient Tragedy*, that is, *to purge the passions by pity and terror*.'[17] Walpole's method for provoking terror is principally that of surprise. He deploys the

---

[16] *The Romantic Novel in England* (Cambridge, Mass., 1972), 35.
[17] *The Works of Alexander Pope*, ed. W. Warburton, 9 vols. (London, 1770), iv. 166.

kind of shock effects, most of them supernatural, that M. G. Lewis would take much further; the episode of the Bleeding Nun from *The Monk* is a notable example. There is very little of the atmospheric scene-painting that Ann Radcliffe was to make her trade mark; although certain scenes, for instance Isabella's underground escape, and Matilda's fatal tryst with Theodore, hint at a talent for the ominous.

Other contemporary readers join Warburton in testifying to the success of Walpole's treatment of the supernatural. The poet and critic Joseph Warton rated the affective power of the helmet and the armoured hand above anything in Ovid or Apuleius.[18] Ann Yearsley's poem 'To the Honorable H——e W——e, on Reading *The Castle of Otranto*, December 1784', signed 'Bianca', reveals a passionate identification with the experiences of the characters:

> The drowsy eye, half-closing to the lid,
> Stares on OTRANTO's walls; grim terrors rise
> The horrid helmet strikes my soul unbid

Walter Scott, representing a later generation of readers, reaffirmed 'the high merit of many of the marvellous incidents in the romance', and noted that the 'apparition of the skeleton hermit to the Prince of Vicenza was long accounted a masterpiece of the horrible'.[19]

But *Otranto*'s apparitions have also come in for some severe handling, not least by William Hazlitt: 'The great hand and arm, which are thrust into the court-yard, and remain there all day long, are the pasteboard machinery of a pantomime ... They are a matter-of-fact impossibility; a fixture, and no longer a phantom.'[20] Even admirers such as Clara Reeve and Scott were forced to confess that the ceaseless parade of horrors had a diminishing effect; like Manfred

---

[18] *Essay on the Genius and Writings of Pope*, 2 vols. (London, 1762–82), ii. 49–50.
[19] *The Lives of the Novelists* (London, [1925]), 201.
[20] *Lectures on the English Comic Writers, The Complete Works of William Hazlitt*, ed. P. P. Howe, vi (London, 1931), 127.

faced with the arrival of a gigantic sword, the reader becomes 'almost hardened to preternatural appearances'.

One alternative to judging *Otranto* a failure as terror
fiction is to read it as a self-conscious burlesque.[21] Walpole
certainly acknowledged the laughable side of his creation in
various self-deprecating remarks to friends, but at the same
time he betrayed a desire to elicit pity, an aim of classical
tragedy. He writes modestly to Elie de Beaumont: 'If I
make you laugh, for I cannot flatter myself that I shall make
you cry, I shall be content.'[22] Thomas Gray assured him,
maybe teasingly, that on first reading it with some friends at
Cambridge, 'some of us cried a little'.[23] Perhaps the rapid
sale of the first edition gave him the courage of his convic-
tions, for to the second edition he added a poem dedicating
the work to Lady Mary Coke which emphasizes pathos to
the exclusion of both laughter and fear. Particularly telling
in this respect are the changes made in the direction of
sentimentality by Robert Jephson, in the dramatic adapta-
tion *The Count of Narbonne* (1781), to which Walpole gave
his full approval. The supernatural is entirely removed, as
are the comic servants (Bianca, for instance, becomes the
grave and sentimental Jacqueline). Most of the characters
become more straightforwardly virtuous, while the inner
struggle of the Count is highlighted. The play had a successful run at Covent Garden in 1781, and was staged in Dublin
in 1781–2 with John Philip Kemble in the leading role.

This notion of *The Castle of Otranto* as a tear-jerker,
cherished by Walpole and apparently shared by at least
some of the contemporary audience, should serve as a
warning against the assumption that its significance is all
openly accessible to the modern reader. We may feel ourselves expert judges of Gothic fantasy, educated not only

---

[21] The view taken by Elizabeth Napier, *The Failure of Gothic* (Oxford, 1987), 78–82.

[22] *Walpole's Correspondence*, 40. 380 (18 Mar. 1765).

[23] Ibid. 14. 137 (30 Dec. 1764).

by the currently flourishing literature of horror and supernaturalism but also by film and television. Yet there is no reason to assume that because genre conventions persist, their meaning has remained unchanged. To view *Otranto* primarily as a founding text is to conclude that it is a failure, or at best an indication of things to come. It may be worth while, then, to put aside for a moment the presuppositions of genre criticism, and to try to reassess the significance of the work as the product of a very different historical moment, influenced by unfamiliar cultural and political concerns.

One of the most basic assumptions about fantasy today is that it serves as an escape from reality. This idea is reinforced, of course, by the fact that the consumption of fantasy commodities is normally restricted to leisure-time, separate from the 'real' world of work. Walpole, as we have seen, described in a letter how glad he was to immerse himself in the writing of *Otranto* and think about 'anything rather than politics'. This reference to his activities as a Member of Parliament appears to fall in readily enough with our conventional wisdom, and is generally left at that. But the relation between fantasy and reality in the late eighteenth century, and in the case of Walpole in particular, was in fact far more complicated, and can serve as the starting-point for a historically informed reading of the novel.

A central tenet of the theory of the novel in the eighteenth century was the existence of a functional link between fiction and social reality. Novelists in their prefaces routinely cited Horace's motto *utile dulci*: their works would both please and instruct. Imitation was the key. By emulating nature, fiction was able to play the useful role of teaching readers about the world and the moral problems to be faced there, and this educative purpose would redeem its intrinsic falseness. *The Castle of Otranto* obviously represented a challenge to the didactic principle, but a challenge mitigated by the terms of the second Preface. When Walpole insists that the story is a *blend* of the marvellous on the one hand, and of nature and probability on the other, he attempts to bring his story within the bounds of existing literary theory. Unlikely though it may seem to us that *Otranto* could teach any lesson relevant to modern life, this was nevertheless the corollary of making the characters 'think, speak and act, as it might be supposed mere men and women would do in extraordinary situations'. And although in the first Preface Walpole a.k.a. William Marshall complains that the author could find no 'more useful moral than this; that *the sins of the fathers are visited on their children to the third and fourth generation*', Eleanor Fenn, under the pseudonym of 'Mrs Teachwell', wrote two essays on the novel for the *Female Guardian* asserting that the 'whole volume is replete with refined morality', and selected some passages to include in an anthology of improving literature for the young.[24]

But fantasy is also brought into relation with social reality in another, more disturbing way by the subtitling of *Otranto* as a 'Gothic story'. We have already encountered Richard Hurd as an apologist for the literature of the gothic era: in *Letters on Chivalry and Romance* he challenged the conventional ridicule of 'the ages, we call barbarous', and drew on recent French scholarship in order to explain cultural forms as the logical outcome of a feudal social order. Thus tales of enchantment, with all their apparent irrationality, 'shadowed out' the realities of their times: giants 'were oppressive feudal Lords, and every Lord was to be met with, like the Giant, in his strong hold, or castle', and their wretched and equally violent dependants 'were the Savages of Romance'.[25]

[24] See Peter Sabor (ed.), *Horace Walpole: The Critical Heritage* (London and New York, 1987), 81–2.

[25] *Letters on Chivalry and Romance*, ed. and introd. H. Trowbridge, 1st edn. facsimile (Los Angeles, 1963), 28–9.

The concept of romance as social allegory made the literature of the past at once comprehensible and palatable for the enlightened reader. It followed that eighteenth-century society must have its own characteristic style of literary production and, given that this society is peaceful, commercial, civilized, well ordered, it ought to produce nothing but 'polite' literature. From this historicist perspective, Walpole's airy proposal to combine ancient and modern romance is not only monstrous, but transgressive. If the conventions of ancient romance can be revived with success by modern authors, then what does that say about the present? *Otranto* and other pioneering Gothic romances tended to generate anxiety and provoke denunciation from the critics because they implied that there must be something awry in the contemporary social order itself. A Gothic revival in literature disturbed the comfortable vision of historical progress.

For an idea of the kind of social and political issues involved in the production of Gothic romance, we cannot do better than return to the biography of Walpole himself. His career illustrates, reciprocally, the role Gothic fantasy could play in eighteenth-century politics. As the son of a Prime Minister, he was early initiated into the mysteries of the trade. Still abroad on the Grand Tour, he was elected an MP at the age of 24. However, his entrance into Parliament coincided with his father's fall from power, and the trappings of high state which had surrounded him in childhood and early youth vanished. Robert Walpole's death followed soon after in 1744, but his son remained conscious of former glory and was determined to uphold the Whig principles as a kind of family legacy. For twenty-seven years he attended debates in the House of Commons although, not being much of a public speaker, he intervened on only a few occasions. His forte, as he freely admitted, was faction and backstairs intrigue. He minutely details this kind of activity in his political *Memoirs*, published posthumously, which have since become a vital source of information for historians of the Georgian political scene.

Walpole often spoke of Strawberry Hill as a haven from the life of politics and hectic socializing which he continued to lead intermittently in London. But as a letter to George Montagu suggests, the exercise of his antiquarian tastes was not restricted to his Twickenham retreat:

You will think me very fickle and that I have but a slight regard to the castle (I am building) of my ancestors, when you hear that I have been these last eight days in London amid dust and stinks, instead of syringa, roses, battlements and niches; but you perhaps recollect that I have another Gothic passion, which is for squabbles in the Wittenagemot [*sic*]. I can't say the contests have run so high in either house, as they have sometimes done in former days, but this age has found a new method of parliamentary altercations. The Commons abuse the Barons, and the Barons return it.[26]

According to Whig historiography, the Anglo-Saxon Witenagemot was the forerunner of the modern Parliament, embodying an ideal balance of power shared by monarch, lords, and commoners known as the 'Gothic Constitution'. Disruption of this balance gave rise to the tumultuous events of the seventeenth century: the Civil War, the establishment of a Commonwealth followed by Restoration of the Stuart line, the deposing of James II, and finally the installation of the Protestant William of Orange and Queen Mary. The Whig party were the chief supporters and beneficiaries of this last 'Glorious Revolution' of 1688, and set themselves up as guardians of the Constitution against any threat from the Jacobites in exile abroad, or any suspected extension of the royal prerogative at home. Walpole, with all the force of his lively imagination, identified with the cause, declaring himself 'a Whig to the backbone'.[27] He arranged around his bed the trophies of limited monarchy:

---

[26] *Walpole's Correspondence*, 9. 149 (11 May 1753).
[27] Ibid. 37. 406 (letter to Conway, 23 Sept. 1755).

a copy of the Magna Carta on one side, the warrant for the execution of Charles I on the other. The Gothic castle at Strawberry Hill was itself a monument to a life in which fantasy and politics were inextricably combined.

For Walpole, politics could never be merely a question of party allegiance; it was a matter of blood, of dynasty. He took great pride in the achievements of his family and of none more than his cousin Henry Seymour Conway, three years his junior, whom he regarded as the natural heir to his father's mantle. Conway was handsome, intelligent, principled, a successful soldier and a capable politician. Walpole admired him unreservedly, and as always in his likings, he gave his fancy free play. In a letter to Conway himself he playfully describes him as a figure out of an antique romance, in terms remarkably similar to the portrait of Alfonso in *The Castle of Otranto*:

Elmodorus was tall and perfectly well made, his face oval, and features regularly handsome, but not effeminate; his complexion sentimentally brown, with not much colour; his teeth fine, and forehead agreeably low, round which his black hair curled naturally and beautifully. His eyes were black too, but had nothing fierce or insolent; on the contrary, a certain melancholy swimmingness that described hopeless love, rather than a natural amorous languish.[28]

On another occasion he marvels at Conway's resemblance to a medieval knight as he tries on an old helmet found in a gothic church: 'you can't imagine how it suited him, how antique and handsome he looked';[29] again there is an interesting foreshadowing of *Otranto*. This intense attachment has been attributed to romantic or sexual feelings on Walpole's part, but it seems clear that in reveries of this kind he sees Conway above all as a chivalrous champion of the Walpoles and of the Whigs.

[28] Ibid. 37. 261 (24 Oct. 1746 OS).
[29] Ibid. 9. 102 (to George Montagu, 28 Sept. 1749).

At no time was the link between Walpole's two 'Gothic passions' more apparent than in the spring of 1764. During the preceding year he had involved himself in the political crisis of the moment to a greater extent than ever before. The cause was the arrest of the MP and journalist John Wilkes for libelling the King in the satirical journal, the *North Briton*. His imprisonment provoked violent popular protest in London over the use of General Warrants by the Government to suppress free speech. In the Commons, debate centred on the violation of Parliamentary privilege in Wilkes's case; for the Whigs in opposition it was an opportunity to rehearse all the favourite arguments against unbridled royal authority. Walpole's correspondence of the time and his *Memoirs of the Reign of George III* are evidence of the pitch of emotion to which this episode provoked him.

His interest was considerably heightened by Conway's role in the affair. In April 1763 Conway had returned from his post as commander of a regiment in Germany. In November, influenced by Walpole, he had voted against the Government over the question of court privilege. After a tense hiatus, in April 1764 he was summarily dismissed from his military command, and from a civil post as Groom of the Bedchamber. The impact on Walpole was tremendous: at first he refused to believe the news, but once he was persuaded of it he retired to Strawberry Hill in an attempt to recover his self-control. He immediately offered Conway the whole of his fortune in recompense and threw himself into efforts, as he states, to bring down the Government. Only with the creation of a Whig administration could Conway's fortunes be restored. In early June, Walpole responded to an anonymous pamphlet supporting the Government's treatment of Conway with *A Counter-Address to the Public, on the Late Dismission of a General Officer*, representing his grievances in the most elevated terms and insisting that the public love the Man, who was ready to sacrifice to the Liberties of his country those Emoluments which he had obtained by defending it against its domestic and foreign Enemies. They regard him as a Martyr to their Freedom, and to his own conscience ... [and] they will detest a Scribler who defends, recommends, Punishments for Integrity ... Away with *Magna Charta*, the Bill of Rights, & the Revolution [of 1688], if men dare utter this Language in the Face of Day.

This would eventually provoke another pamphlet from the Government hack (the journalist and critic William Guthrie), *A Reply to the Counter-Address*, an extremely personal attack on Walpole, mainly on the score of his affection for Conway. Walpole, by now a confirmed bachelor, is arraigned for the 'effeminacy' of his defence of his cousin, which is taken to betray an unhealthy adoration well known in fashionable circles: 'One of the beaux esprits of the present times, has christened this regard, calling it, with a feigned concern, "an unsuccessful passion, during the course of 20 years".' In addition, he is accused of being an 'old Walpoleian', still scaremongering about the Jacobite threat. Walpole sent a copy to Conway, with the dignified comment: 'They have nothing better to say than that I am in love with you ... I am a very constant old swain: they might have made the years above thirty; it is so long I have had the same unalterable friendship for you, independent of being near relations and bred up together.'[30] Around the same time he suffered one of the severe attacks of gout that tended to flare up at times of emotional crisis.

It was in the midst of this 'political frenzy' (as his friend Gilly Williams described it) that Walpole produced his most successful creative effort; that is to say, during a period in which he was entertaining apocalyptic visions of the future, rather than dwelling nostalgically on the past. As he writes in the *Memoirs*, he fully expected the outbreak of

---

[30] *Walpole's Correspondence*, 38. 437 (1 Sept. 1764).

civil war: 'My nature shuddered at the thought of blood.'[31] Against this background, Walpole's dream occurred, of a gigantic hand in armour, resting on the uppermost banister of a staircase. In terms of Whig demonology, the armoured hand connotes an arbitrary, executive power; its appearance in a scene resembling Strawberry Hill implies an invasion into Walpole's affairs. Whatever the unconscious origins of the dream might have been, once Walpole had awakened he was left with an image which could not fail to arouse the deepest interests of his conscious mind. It provided the raw material on which his politicized imagination went to work, and the stark emblem of power was mediated by a narrative expansion. In isolation, it suggested the helplessness of the beholder; in the context of the novel it provides the opportunity for a humorous subversion of authority. The dream-vision was incorporated in the final chapter and described in the words of Bianca: 'I looked up, and . . . I saw upon the uppermost banister of the great stairs a hand in armour as big, as big—I thought I should have swooned.' In her terror, she exposes Manfred's attempts to obtain information by bribery, and puts Frederic on his guard against him.

Although at one level *Otranto* could be read as an attempt to exorcize political demons by reworking and containing them within an amusing and fantastical story, there is another level at which the representation of power remains troublingly open and unresolved. Once we get beyond spotting Gothic conventions, the central logic of the story becomes apparent: the control of property over people. The theme is evoked not by *blending* the marvellous and the natural, but rather by utilizing the gulf between them to dramatic effect. The supernatural phenomena in the narrative are emanations of a providential law of inheritance. The characters, on the other hand, are guided by the law of human nature, as it was then conceived (with the

---

[31] *Memoirs of the Reign of King George the Third*, ed. G. F. Russell Barker, 4 vols. (London, 1894), ii. 2.

inclusion of a good deal more formal diction and sensibility than seems natural to the modern reader). The two laws perpetually clash, but the former will prevail, with tragic consequences. It is typical that the intervention of the hand on the staircase reminds Frederic of his claims to the title of Otranto, and checks his spontaneous desire for Matilda.

The principality of Otranto has become separated by criminal means from its rightful possessors. And now, after two generations (having been delayed by a bribe to St Nicholas), supernatural forces take shape to effect a restoration. But the conclusion goes beyond a simple righting of wrongs: for those punished are innocent of the original crime, and nobody is satisfied by the final dispensation. The demands of property inheritance are inimical to human happiness: this is the message of numerous sentimental fictions of the period, beginning with Richardson's *Clarissa*. Far from being a problem restricted to the feudal past, or to the pages of romance, this was a live issue, bearing on the conflict between aristocratic and bourgeois ideals of social being.

The doctrine of the divine right of kings was the ultimate form of providential property-holding; but this was a superstition of which the great Whig Lords had managed to disabuse themselves in 1688 (though as we have seen, Walpole was ever on his guard against it). In its place they established a cult of landed wealth as the foundation of aristocratic hegemony. Legal provisions for maintaining the integrity of estates were strengthened in response to the rising fortunes of the trading classes. Primogeniture had, of course, long been the rule. But it was beginning to be viewed by middle-class critics as an artificial imposition, which militated against the rights and the happiness of individuals. Adam Smith contrasts 'the natural law of succession' which divides property among all the children of the family, with the law of primogeniture, 'contrary to nature, to reason, and to justice', which arose out of the exigencies of feudal times, and has been maintained, irrationally, into the present.[32] The device of 'strict settlement' was introduced to prevent heirs selling off portions of their estate to suit their own interests. The preservation of property was all. As Henry Home writes of the law of entail, it enabled 'every land-proprietor to fetter his estate for ever; to tyrannize over his heirs'; property becomes 'in effect a mortmain', literally speaking, the dead hand of the past weighing on the present.[33]

Walpole was no radical, nor was he remotely middle class, but in *The Castle of Otranto* he brings into play the incongruities most likely to move and terrify the audience of his day. The hand of the past is not only dead, it is also, like most of the other apparitions, enormous. This is not hyperbole; it indicates disproportionate forces. Location is also significant: a hand appears on a staircase, a helmet in the courtyard, a leg in the doorway. The passage, and metaphorically the will, of the living is blocked by the intentions of the dead. With regard to the prevailing laws of property inheritance, Walpole's personal view, as might be expected of a third son, was sceptical. Elsewhere he dealt with the theme less portentously. Inspired by a suggestion that the inheritance of Strawberry Hill should be legally settled, he wrote 'The Entail; A Fable', in which a butterfly, having taken up residency in a rose, settles the family's ownership in perpetuity: 'Each leaf he binds, each bud he ties | To eggs of eggs of BUTTERFLIES'.[34]

In so far as *The Castle of Otranto* is a novel of sensibility, it is allied with the contemporary critique of aristocratic institutions. As a work of terror, it invites the reader to revel in the nightmarish collapse of a system of power that con-

---

[32] *An Inquiry into the Nature and Causes of the Wealth of Nations*, 2 vols. (Oxford, 1976), i. 382; *Lectures on Jurisprudence*, cit. 383 n. 6.

[33] *Sketches of the History of Man*, 2 vols. (Edinburgh and London, 1774), ii. 481–3.

[34] *The Works of Horatio Walpole* (London, 1798–1825), i. 28–9.

tains the seeds of its own destruction. Many years after it was written, Walpole, now bearing the title of Earl of Orford, was to be severely shaken by the events of the French Revolution; perhaps he saw in them a sequel to his dream, a terrible revenge of the forces of the present over those of the past: regicide; the dispossession, exile, and slaughter of the aristocracy; power unbalanced, tipping violently from the King to the third estate. Certainly he reflected on his own career as a 'quiet republican', and repented. And before his death in 1797, he must also have observed somewhat ruefully the simultaneous explosion of revolutionary politics and the genre he himself had initiated. A letter he wrote to Lady Ossory, expressing his dismay at the execution of Louis XVI and the start of the Reign of Terror, might equally well allude to his own part in the evolution of a new literary discourse of the unspeakable: 'It remained for the enlightened eighteenth century to baffle language and invent horrors that can be found in no vocabulary.'[35]

[35] *Walpole's Correspondence* (letter to Lady Ossory, 29 Jan. 1793).

# NOTE ON THE TEXT

THE text followed here is that in the *Works of Horatio Walpole, Earl of Orford* (London, 1798), ii. 1–90, which corrects the typographical errors of the earlier editions and is the last text of the novel that the author prepared for the press. The first edition of 500 copies appeared on 24 December 1764 (although the title-page carried the date of 1765); the second (of the same number of copies), on 11 April 1765. The third was in 1766, the fourth in 1782, the fifth in 1786, and the sixth (a reprint of the fifth) in 1791. Another edition (also known as the sixth) was printed at Parma in 1791 by Bodoni for Edwards. Others came in 1793 (two editions), 1794, 1796, and 1797. French translations were published in 1767 and 1797 and Italian translations in 1794 and 1795. For complete bibliographical notes and description, see A. T. Hazen, *A Bibliography of Horace Walpole* (New Haven, 1948), 52–67.

# SELECT BIBLIOGRAPHY

Baldick Chris, (ed.), *The Oxford Book of Gothic Tales* (Oxford and New York, 1992).

Clery, E. J., *The Rise of Supernatural Fiction, 1762–1800* (Cambridge, 1995).

Guest, Harriet, 'The Wanton Muse: Politics and Gender in Gothic Theory After 1760', in Stephen Copley and John Whale (eds.), *Beyond Romanticism: New Approaches to Texts and Contexts, 1780–1832* (London and New York, 1992), 118–39.

Harfst, Betsy Perteit, *Horace Walpole and the Unconscious: An Experiment in Freudian Analysis* (New York, 1980).

Henderson, Andrea, '"An Embarrassing Subject": Use Value and Exchange Value in Early Gothic Characterisation', in Mary A. Favret and Nicola J. Watson (eds.), *At the Limits of Romanticism* (Bloomington, Ind. and Indianapolis, 1994), 225–45.

Hogle, Jerrold E., 'The Ghost of the Counterfeit in the Genesis of the Gothic', in Allan Lloyd Smith and Victor Sage (eds.), *Gothick Origins and Innovations* (Amsterdam and Atlanta, 1994), 23–33.

Kallich, Martin, *Horace Walpole* (New York, 1971).

Ketton-Cremer, R. W., *Horace Walpole: A Biography* (London, 1940).

Kiely, Robert, *The Romantic Novel in England* (Cambridge, Mass., 1972).

Kliger, Samuel, *The Goths in England: A Study in Seventeenth and Eighteenth Century Thought* (Cambridge, Mass., 1952).

Levy, Maurice, *Le Roman 'Gothique' anglais, 1764–1824* (Toulouse, 1968).

Miles, Robert, *Gothic Writing, 1750–1820: A Genealogy* (London and New York, 1993).

Napier, Elizabeth, *The Failure of Gothic* (Oxford, 1987).

Punter, David, *The Literature of Terror* (London, 1980).

Sabor, Peter (ed.), *Horace Walpole: The Critical Heritage* (London and New York, 1987).

Sedgwick, Eve Kosofsky, *The Coherence of Gothic Conventions* (New York, 1986).

Simpson, David B., 'Gothic Sublimity', *New Literary History*, 16: 2 (Winter 1985), 299–319.

Smith, R. J., *The Gothic Bequest: Medieval Institutions in British Thought, 1688–1863* (Cambridge, 1987).

Varma, Devendra P., *The Gothic Flame* (London, 1957).

Watt, Ian, 'Time and the Family in the Gothic Novel: *The Castle of Otranto*', *Eighteenth Century Life*, 10: 3 (1986), 159–71.

Yvon, Paul, *La Vie d'un dilettante: Horace Walpole (1717–1797)* (Paris and London, 1924).

# CHRONOLOGY OF HORACE WALPOLE
# FOURTH EARL OF ORFORD

An extended summary of his life to 1779, drawn up by himself, will be found in the Yale edition of *Horace Walpole's Correspondence*, 13. 1–51.

1717    Born 24 September, OS, in Arlington Street, London, the third surviving son of Sir Robert Walpole and Catherine Shorter.

1727–34    Eton.

1735–9    King's College, Cambridge.

1737    Lady Walpole dies; shortly afterwards Sir Robert marries his mistress, Maria Skerrett, who dies in 1738.

1739–41    Takes Thomas Gray, his intimate friend at Eton and Cambridge, on the Grand Tour to France and Italy. He has already begun writing the letters on which his fame chiefly rests.

1741    Elected to Parliament for a family borough in Cornwall while still abroad. His places in the Exchequer, secured for him by his father, rise in time to as much as £5,000 a year.

1742    Sir Robert resigns as Prime Minister and is created Earl of Orford; his last three years are spent chiefly at Houghton, his house in Norfolk.

1747    Horace Walpole's first book, *Aedes Walpolianae*, an account of the pictures at Houghton, published.

1747    Leases Strawberry Hill, Twickenham.

1749    Buys Strawberry Hill and begins to remodel it in the Gothic manner.

1751    Begins writing his *Memoirs*, which he continues to 1791.

1755    First attack of gout, to which he becomes a martyr.

1757    Erects a private printing press at Strawberry Hill, where he brings out books and ephemera until 1789. These include his own *Catalogue of Royal and Noble Authors*, 2 vols. (1758), *Anecdotes of Painting in England*, 5 vols. (1762–80), and *The Mysterious Mother* (a tragedy) (1768).

1764    24 December, *The Castle of Otranto* published.

1768    *Historic Doubts on the Life and Reign of King Richard the Third* published; retires from Parliament.

1777    Unfairly charged with contributing to Chatterton's death.

1791    5 December, succeeds his nephew as 4th Earl of Orford.

1797    Dies, unmarried, at his home in Berkeley Square in his eightieth year.

# THE
# CASTLE of OTRANTO,
# A
# STORY.

Translated by

## WILLIAM MARSHAL, Gent.

From the Original ITALIAN of

## ONUPHRIO MURALTO,

CANON of the Church of St. NICHOLAS
at OTRANTO.

## LONDON:

Printed for THO. LOWNDS in Fleet-Street.
MDCCLXV.

*Title-page of the first edition*

# THE

# CASTLE of OTRANTO,

# A

# GOTHIC STORY.

——— *Vanæ*
*Fingentur species, tamen ut Pes, & Caput uni*
*Reddantur formæ.* ———

HOR.

## THE SECOND EDITION.

*LONDON:*
Printed for WILLIAM BATHOE in the *Strand,*
and THOMAS LOWNDS in *Fleet-Street.*

M. DCC. LXV.

*Title-page of the second edition*

# PREFACE

## TO THE FIRST EDITION

THE following work was found in the library of an ancient catholic family in the north of England. It was printed at Naples, in the black letter,* in the year 1529. How much sooner it was written does not appear. The principal incidents are such as were believed in the darkest ages of christianity; but the language and conduct have nothing that favours of barbarism. The style is the purest Italian.* If the story was written near the time when it is supposed to have happened, it must have been between 1095, the æra of the first crusade, and 1243, the date of the last, or not long afterwards.* There is no other circumstance in the work that can lead us to guess at the period in which the scene is laid: the names of the actors are evidently fictitious, and probably disguised on purpose: yet the Spanish names of the domestics seem to indicate that this work was not composed until the establishment of the Arragonian kings in Naples* had made Spanish appellations familiar in that country. The beauty of the diction, and the zeal of the author, [moderated however by singular judgment] concur to make me think that the date of the composition was little antecedent to that of the impression. Letters were then in their most flourishing state in Italy, and contributed to dispel the empire of superstition, at that time so forcibly attacked by the reformers. It is not unlikely that an artful priest might endeavour to turn their own arms on the innovators; and might avail himself of his abilities as an author to confirm the populace in their ancient errors and superstitions. If this was his view, he has certainly acted with signal address. Such a work as the following would enslave a hundred vulgar minds beyond half the books of controversy that have been written from the days of Luther to the present hour.

The solution of the author's motives is however offered as a mere conjecture. Whatever his views were, or whatever effects the execution of them might have, his work can only be laid before the public at present as a matter of entertainment. Even as such, some apology for it is necessary. Miracles, visions, necromancy, dreams, and other preternatural events, are exploded now even from romances. That was not the case when our author wrote; much less when the story itself is supposed to have happened. Belief in every kind of prodigy was so established in those dark ages, that an author would not be faithful to the *manners* of the times who should omit all mention of them. He is not bound to believe them himself, but he must represent his actors as believing them.

If this *air* of the *miraculous* is excused, the reader will find nothing else unworthy of his perusal. Allow the possibility of the facts, and all the actors comport themselves as persons would do in their situation. There is no bombast, no similies, flowers, digressions, or unnecessary descriptions. Every thing tends directly to the catastrophe. Never is the reader's attention relaxed. The rules of the drama* are almost observed throughout the conduct of the piece. The characters are well drawn, and still better maintained. Terror, the author's principal engine, prevents the story from ever languishing; and it is so often contrasted by pity, that the mind is kept up in a constant vicissitude of interesting passions.

Some persons may perhaps think the characters of the domestics too little serious for the general cast of the story; but besides their opposition to the principal personages, the art of the author is very observable in his conduct of the subalterns. They discover many passages essential to the story, which could not well be brought to light but by their *naïveté* and simplicity: in particular, the womanish terror and foibles of Bianca, in the last chapter, conduce essentially towards advancing the catastrophe.

It is natural for a translator to be prejudiced in favour of his adopted work. More impartial readers may not be so much struck with the beauties of this piece as I was. Yet I am not blind to my author's defects. I could wish he had grounded his plan on a more useful moral than this; that *the sins of fathers are visited on their children to the third and fourth generation*. I doubt whether in his time, any more than at present, ambition curbed its appetite of dominion from the dread of so remote a punishment. And yet this moral is weakened by that less direct insinuation, that even such anathema may be diverted by devotion to saint Nicholas.* Here the interest of the monk plainly gets the better of the judgment of the author. However, with all its faults, I have no doubt but the English reader will be pleased with a sight of this performance. The piety that reigns throughout, the lessons of virtue that are inculcated, and the rigid purity of the sentiments, exempt this work from the censure to which romances are but too liable. Should it meet with the success I hope for, I may be encouraged to re-print the original Italian, though it will tend to depreciate my own labour. Our language falls far short of the charms of the Italian, both for variety and harmony. The latter is peculiarly excellent for simple narrative. It is difficult in English *to relate* without falling too low or rising too high; a fault obviously occasioned by the little care taken to speak pure language in common conversation. Every Italian or Frenchman of any rank piques himself on speaking his own tongue correctly and with choice. I cannot flatter myself with having done justice to my author in this respect: his style is as elegant as his conduct of the passions is masterly. It is pity that he did not apply his talents to what they were evidently proper for, the theatre.

I will detain the reader no longer but to make one short remark. Though the machinery is invention, and the names of the actors imaginary, I cannot but believe that the groundwork of the story is founded on truth. The scene is undoubtedly laid in some real castle.\* The author seems frequently, without design, to describe particular parts. *The chamber*, says he, *on the right hand; the door on the left hand; the distance from the chapel to Conrad's apartment*: these and other passages are strong presumptions that the author had some certain building in his eye. Curious persons, who have leisure to employ in such researches, may possibly discover in the Italian writers the foundation on which our author has built. If a catastrophe, at all resembling that which he describes, is believed to have given rise to this work, it will contribute to interest the reader, and will make *The Castle of Otranto* a still more moving story.

# PREFACE

## TO THE SECOND EDITION

THE favourable manner in which this little piece has been received by the public, calls upon the author to explain the grounds on which he composed it. But before he opens those motives, it is fit that he should ask pardon of his readers for having offered his work to them under the borrowed personage of a translator. As diffidence of his own abilities, and the novelty of the attempt, were his sole inducements to assume that disguise, he flatters himself he shall appear excusable. He resigned his performance to the impartial judgment of the public; determined to let it perish in obscurity, if disapproved; nor meaning to avow such a trifle, unless better judges should pronounce that he might own it without a blush.

It was an attempt to blend the two kinds of romance,* the ancient and the modern. In the former all was imagination and improbability: in the latter, nature is always intended to be, and sometimes has been, copied with success. Invention has not been wanting; but the great resources of fancy have been dammed up, by a strict adherence to common life. But if in the latter species Nature has cramped imagination, she did but take her revenge, having been totally excluded from old romances. The actions, sentiments, conversations, of the heroes and heroines of ancient days were as unnatural as the machines employed to put them in motion.

The author of the following pages thought it possible to reconcile the two kinds. Desirous of leaving the powers of fancy* at liberty to expatiate through the boundless realms of invention, and thence of creating more interesting situations, he wished to conduct the mortal agents in his drama according to the rules of probability;* in short, to make them think, speak and act, as it might be supposed mere men and women would do in extraordinary positions. He had observed, that in all inspired writings, the personages under the dispensation of miracles, and witnesses to the most stupendous phenomena, never lose sight of their human character: whereas in the productions of romantic story, an improbable event never fails to be attended by an absurd dialogue. The actors seem to lose their senses the moment the laws of nature have lost their tone. As the public have applauded the attempt, the author must not say he was entirely unequal to the task he had undertaken: yet if the new route he has struck out shall have paved a road for men of brighter talents, he shall own with pleasure and modesty, that he was sensible the plan was capable of receiving greater embellishments than his imagination or conduct of the passions could bestow on it.

With regard to the deportment of the domestics, on which I have touched in the former preface, I will beg leave to add a few words. The simplicity of their behaviour, almost tending to excite smiles, which at first seem not consonant to the serious cast of the work, appeared to me not only not improper, but was marked designedly in that manner. My rule was nature. However grave, important, or even melancholy, the sensations of princes and heroes may be, they do not stamp the same affections on their domestics: at least the latter do not, or should not be made to express their passions in the same dignified tone. In my humble opinion, the contrast between the sublime of the one, and the *naïveté* of the other, sets the pathetic of the former in a stronger light. The very impatience which a reader feels, while delayed by the coarse pleasantries of vulgar actors from arriving at the knowledge of the important catastrophe he expects, perhaps heightens, certainly proves that he has been artfully interested in, the depending event. But I had higher authority than my own opinion for this conduct. That great master of nature, Shakespeare, was the model I copied.* Let me ask if his tragedies of Hamlet and Julius Caesar would not lose a considerable share of the spirit and wonderful beauties, if the humour of the grave-diggers, the fooleries of Polonius, and the clumsy jests of the Roman citizens were omitted, or vested in heroics?* Is not the eloquence of Antony, the nobler and affectedly unaffected oration of Brutus, artificially exalted by the rude bursts of nature from the mouths of their auditors? These touches remind one of the Grecian sculptor, who, to convey the idea of a Colossus within the dimensions of a seal, inserted a little boy measuring his thumb.[1]

No, says Voltaire* in his edition of Corneille, this mixture of buffoonery and solemnity is intolerable—Voltaire is a genius[1]—but not of Shakespeare's magnitude. Without recurring to disputable authority, I appeal from Voltaire to himself. I shall not avail myself of his former encomiums on our mighty poet; though the French critic has twice translated the same speech in Hamlet, some years ago in admiration, latterly in derision;* and I am sorry to find that his judgment grows weaker, when it ought to be farther matured. But I shall make use of his own words, delivered on

[1] The following remark is foreign to the present question, yet excusable in an Englishman, who is willing to think that the severe criticisms of so masterly a writer as Voltaire on our immortal countryman, may have been the effusions of wit and precipitation, rather than the result of judgment and attention. May not the critic's skill in the force and powers of our language have been as incorrect and incompetent as his knowledge of our history? Of the latter his own pen has dropped glaring evidence. In his preface to Thomas Corneille's Earl of Essex, monsieur de Voltaire allows that the truth of history has been grossly perverted in that piece. In excuse he pleads, that when Corneille wrote, the noblesse of France were much unread in English story; but now, says the commentator, that they study it, such misrepresentation would not be suffered——Yet forgetting that the period of ignorance is lapsed, and that it is not very necessary to instruct the knowing, he undertakes from the overflowing of his own reading to give the nobility of his own country a detail of queen Elizabeth's favourites—of whom, says he, Robert Dudley was the first, and the earl of Leicester the second.——Could one have believed that it could be necessary to inform monsieur de Voltaire himself, that Robert Dudley and the earl of Leicester were the same person?*

the general topic of the theatre, when he was neither thinking to recommend or decry Shakespeare's practice; conse-
quently at a moment when Voltaire was impartial. In the
preface to his Enfant prodigue, that exquisite piece of which
I declare my admiration, and which, should I live twenty
years longer, I trust I should never attempt to ridicule, he
has these words, speaking of comedy, [but equally applica-
ble to tragedy, if tragedy is, as surely it ought to be, a picture
of human life; nor can I conceive why occasional pleasantry
ought more to be banished from the tragic scene, than pathetic seriousness from the comic] On y voit un melange
de serieux et de plaisanterie, de comique et de touchant;
souvent même une seule avanture produit tous ces contrastes.
Rien n'est si commun qu'une maison dans laquelle un pere
gronde, une fille occupée de sa passion pleure; le fils se
moque des deux, et quelques parens prennent part
differemment à la scene, &c. Nous n'inferons pas de là que
toute comedie doive avoir des scenes de bouffonnerie et des
scenes attendrissantes: il y a beaucoup de tres bonnes pieces
où il ne regne que de la gayeté; d'autres toutes serieuses;
d'autres melangées: d'autres où l'attendrissement va jusques
aux larmes: il ne faut donner l'exclusion à aucun genre: et si
l'on me demandoit, quel genre est le meilleur, je repondrois,
celui qui est le mieux traité.* Surely if a comedy may be
toute serieuse, tragedy may now and then, soberly, be indulged in a smile. Who shall proscribe it? Shall the critic,
who in self-defence declares that no kind ought to be excluded from comedy, give laws to Shakespeare?

I am aware that the preface from whence I have quoted
these passages does not stand in monsieur de Voltaire's
name, but in that of his editor; yet who doubts that the
editor and author were the same person? Or where is the
editor, who has so happily possessed himself of his author's
style and brilliant ease of argument? These passages were
indubitably the genuine sentiments of that great writer. In
his epistle to Maffei,* prefixed to his Merope, he delivers

almost the same opinion, though I doubt with a little irony. I will repeat his words, and then give my reason for quoting them. After translating a passage in Maffei's Merope, monsieur de Voltaire adds, *Tous ces traits sont naïfs: tout y est convenable à ceux que vous introduisez sur la scene*, et aux mœurs que vous leur donnez. *Ces familiarités naturelles eussent été, à ce que je crois, bien reçues dans Athenes; mais Paris et notre parterre veulent une autre espece de simplicité.** I doubt, I say, whether there is not a grain of sneer in this and other passages of that epistle; yet the force of truth is not damaged by being tinged with ridicule. Maffei was to represent a Grecian story: surely the Athenians were as competent judges of Grecian manners, and of the propriety of introducing them, as the parterre of Paris. On the contrary, says Voltaire [and I cannot but admire his reasoning] there were but ten thousand citizens at Athens, and Paris has near eight hundred thousand inhabitants, among whom one may reckon thirty thousand judges of dramatic works.—Indeed!—But allowing so numerous a tribunal, I believe this is the only instance in which it was ever pretended that thirty thousand persons, living near two thousand years after the æra in question, were, upon the mere face of the poll, declared better judges than the Grecians themselves of what ought to be the manners of a tragedy written on a Grecian story.

I will not enter into a discussion of the *espece de simplicité*,* which the *parterre** of Paris demands, nor of the shackles with which *the thirty thousand judges* have cramped their poetry, the chief merit of which, as I gather from repeated passages in The New Commentary on Corneille, consists in vaulting in spite of those fetters; a merit which, if true, would reduce poetry from the lofty effort of imagination, to a puerile and most contemptible labour—*difficiles nugæ** with a witness! I cannot help however mentioning a couplet, which to my English ears always sounded as the flattest and most trifling instance of circumstantial propriety; but which Voltaire, who has dealt so severely with nine parts in ten of Corneille's works, has singled out to defend in Racine;*

> *De son appartement cette porte est prochaine,*
> *Et cette autre conduit dans celui de la reine.*

In English,

> To Cæsar's *closet through this door you come,*
> *And t'other leads to the queen's drawing-room.*

Unhappy Shakespeare! hadst thou made Rosencrans inform his compeer Guildenstern of the ichnography* of the palace of Copenhagen, instead of presenting us with a moral dialogue between the prince of Denmark and the grave-digger, the illuminated pit of Paris would have been instructed a *second time** to adore thy talents.

The result of all I have said is to shelter my own daring under the cannon of the brightest genius this country, at least, has produced. I might have pleaded, that having created a new species of romance, I was at liberty to lay down what rules I thought fit for the conduct of it: but I should be more proud of having imitated, however faintly, weakly, and at a distance, so masterly a pattern, than to enjoy the entire merit of invention, unless I could have marked my work with genius as well as with originality. Such as it is, the public have honoured it sufficiently, whatever rank their suffrages allot to it.*

# SONNET

## LADY MARY COKE*

THE gentle maid, whose hapless tale
These melancholy pages speak;
Say, gracious lady, shall she fail
To draw the tear adown thy cheek?

No; never was thy pitying breast
Insensible to human woes;
Tender, though firm, it melts distrest
For weaknesses it never knows.

Oh! guard the marvels I relate
Of fell ambition scourg'd by fate,
   From reason's peevish blame:
Blest with thy smile, my dauntless sail
I dare expand to fancy's gale,
   For sure thy smiles are fame.

H. W.

# THE CASTLE OF OTRANTO

*A Gothic Story**

## CHAPTER I

MANFRED, prince of Otranto, had one son and one daughter: the latter, a most beautiful virgin, aged eighteen, was called Matilda. Conrad, the son, was three years younger, a homely youth, sickly, and of no promising disposition; yet he was the darling of his father, who never showed any symptoms of affection to Matilda. Manfred had contracted a marriage for his son with the marquis of Vicenza's daughter, Isabella; and she had already been delivered by her guardians into the hands of Manfred, that he might celebrate the wedding as soon as Conrad's infirm state of health would permit. Manfred's impatience for this ceremonial was remarked by his family and neighbours. The former, indeed, apprehending the severity of their prince's disposition, did not dare to utter their surmises on this precipitation. Hippolita, his wife, an amiable lady, did sometimes venture to represent the danger of marrying their only son so early, considering his great youth, and greater infirmities; but she never received any other answer than reflections on her own sterility, who had given him but one heir. His tenants and subjects were less cautious in their discourses: they attributed this hasty wedding to the prince's dread of seeing accomplished an ancient prophecy, which was said to have pronounced, *That the castle and lordship of Otranto should pass from the present family, whenever the real owner should be grown too large to inhabit it.* It was difficult to make any sense of this prophecy; and still less easy to conceive what it had to do with the marriage in question. Yet these mysteries, or contradictions, did not make the populace adhere the less to their opinion.

Young Conrad's birth-day was fixed for his espousals. The company was assembled in the chapel of the castle, and every thing ready for beginning the divine office, when Conrad himself was missing. Manfred, impatient of the least delay, and who had not observed his son retire, dispatched one of his attendants to summon the young prince. The servant, who had not staid long enough to have crossed the court to Conrad's apartment, came running back breathless, in a frantic manner, his eyes staring, and foaming at the mouth. He said nothing, but pointed to the court. The company were struck with terror and amazement. The princess Hippolita, without knowing what was the matter, but anxious for her son, swooned away. Manfred, less apprehensive than enraged at the procrastination of the nuptials, and at the folly of his domestic, asked imperiously, what was the matter? The fellow made no answer, but continued pointing towards the court-yard; and at last, after repeated questions put to him, cried out, Oh, the helmet! the helmet! In the mean time some of the company had run into the court, from whence was heard a confused noise of shrieks, horror, and surprise. Manfred, who began to be alarmed at not seeing his son, went himself to get information of what occasioned this strange confusion. Matilda remained endeavouring to assist her mother, and Isabella staid for the same purpose, and to avoid showing any impatience for the bridegroom, for whom, in truth, she had conceived little affection.

The first thing that struck Manfred's eyes was a group of his servants endeavouring to raise something that appeared to him a mountain of sable plumes. He gazed without believing his sight. What are ye doing? cried Manfred, wrathfully: Where is my son? A volley of voices replied, Oh, my lord! the prince! the prince! the helmet! the helmet! Shocked with these lamentable sounds, and dreading he knew not what, he advanced hastily—But what a sight for a father's eyes!—He beheld his child dashed to pieces, and almost buried under an enormous helmet, an hundred times more large than any casque ever made for human being, and shaded with a proportionable quantity of black feathers.

The horror of the spectacle, the ignorance of all around how this misfortune happened, and above all, the tremendous phænomenon before him, took away the prince's speech. Yet his silence lasted longer than even grief could occasion. He fixed his eyes on what he wished in vain to believe a vision; and seemed less attentive to his loss, than buried in meditation on the stupendous object that had occasioned it. He touched, he examined the fatal casque; nor could even the bleeding mangled remains of the young prince divert the eyes of Manfred from the portent before him. All who had known his partial fondness for young Conrad, were as much surprised at their prince's insensibility, as thunderstruck themselves at the miracle of the helmet. They conveyed the disfigured corpse into the hall, without receiving the least direction from Manfred. As little was he attentive to the ladies who remained in the chapel: on the contrary, without mentioning the unhappy princesses his wife and daughter, the first sounds that dropped from Manfred's lips were, Take care of the lady Isabella.

The domestics, without observing the singularity of this direction, were guided by their affection to their mistress to consider it as peculiarly addressed to her situation, and flew to her assistance. They conveyed her to her chamber more dead than alive, and indifferent to all the strange circumstances she heard, except the death of her son. Matilda, who doted on her mother, smothered her own grief and amazement, and thought of nothing but assisting and comforting her afflicted parent. Isabella, who had been treated by Hippolita like a daughter, and who returned that tenderness with equal duty and affection, was scarce less assiduous about the princess; at the same time endeavouring to partake and lessen the weight of sorrow which she saw Matilda strove to suppress, for whom she had conceived the warmest sympathy of friendship. Yet her own situation could not help finding its place in her thoughts. She felt no concern for the death of young Conrad, except commiseration; and she was not sorry to be delivered from a marriage which had promised her little felicity, either from her destined bridegroom, or from the severe temper of Manfred, who, though he had distinguished her by great indulgence, had imprinted her mind with terror, from his causeless rigour to such amiable princesses as Hippolita and Matilda.

While the ladies were conveying the wretched mother to her bed, Manfred remained in the court, gazing on the ominous casque, and regardless of the crowd which the strangeness of the event had now assembled round him. The few words he articulated tended solely to enquiries, whether any man knew from whence it could have come? Nobody could give him the least information. However, as it seemed to be the sole object of his curiosity, it soon became so to the rest of the spectators, whose conjectures were as absurd and improbable as the catastrophe itself was unprecedented. In the midst of their senseless guesses a young peasant, whom rumour had drawn thither from a neighbouring village, observed that the miraculous helmet was exactly like that on the figure in black marble of Alfonso the Good, one of their former princes, in the church of St. Nicholas. Villain! What sayest thou? cried Manfred, starting from his trance in a tempest of rage, and seizing the young man by the collar: How darest thou utter such treason? Thy life shall pay for it. The spectators, who as little comprehended the cause of the prince's fury as all the rest they had seen, were at a loss to unravel this new circumstance. The young peasant himself was still more astonished, not conceiving how he had offended the prince:

yet recollecting himself, with a mixture of grace and humility, he disengaged himself from Manfred's gripe, and then, with an obeisance which discovered more jealousy of innocence, than dismay, he asked with respect, of what he was guilty! Manfred, more enraged at the vigour, however decently exerted, with which the young man had shaken off his hold, than appeased by his submission, ordered his attendants to seize him, and, if he had not been withheld by his friends whom he had invited to the nuptials, would have poignarded* the peasant in their arms.

During this altercation some of the vulgar spectators had run to the great church which stood near the castle, and came back open-mouthed, declaring the helmet was missing from Alfonso's statue. Manfred, at this news, grew perfectly frantic; and, as if he sought a subject on which to vent the tempest within him, he rushed again on the young peasant, crying, Villain! monster! sorcerer! 'tis thou hast slain my son! The mob, who wanted some object within the scope of their capacities on whom they might discharge their bewildered reasonings, caught the words from the mouth of their lord, and re-echoed, Ay, ay, 'tis he, 'tis he: he has stolen the helmet from good Alfonso's tomb, and dashed out the brains of our young prince with it:—never reflecting how enormous the disproportion was between the marble helmet that had been in the church, and that of steel before their eyes; nor how impossible it was for a youth, seemingly not twenty, to wield a piece of armour of so prodigious a weight.

The folly of these ejaculations brought Manfred to himself: yet whether provoked at the peasant having observed the resemblance between the two helmets, and thereby led to the farther discovery of the absence of that in the church; or wishing to bury any fresh rumour under so impertinent a supposition; he gravely pronounced that the young man was certainly a necromancer, and that till the church could take cognizance of the affair, he would have the magician, whom they had thus detected, kept prisoner under the helmet itself, which he ordered his attendants to raise, and place the young man under it; declaring he should be kept there without food, with which his own infernal art might furnish him.

It was in vain for the youth to represent against this preposterous sentence: in vain did Manfred's friends endeavour to divert him from this savage and ill-grounded resolution. The generality were charmed with their lord's decision, which to their apprehensions carried great appearance of justice, as the magician was to be punished by the very instrument with which he had offended: nor were they struck with the least compunction at the probability of the youth being starved, for they firmly believed that by his diabolical skill he could easily supply himself with nutriment.

Manfred thus saw his commands even cheerfully obeyed; and appointing a guard with strict orders to prevent any food being conveyed to the prisoner, he dismissed his friends and attendants, and retired to his own chamber, after locking the gates of the castle, in which he suffered none but his domestics to remain.

In the mean time, the care and zeal of the young ladies had brought the princess Hippolita to herself, who amidst the transports of her own sorrow frequently demanded news of her lord, would have dismissed her attendants to watch over him, and at last enjoined Matilda to leave her, and visit and comfort her father. Matilda, who wanted no affectionate duty to Manfred, though she trembled at his austerity, obeyed the orders of Hippolita, whom she tenderly recommended to Isabella; and enquiring of the domestics for her father, was informed that he was retired to his chamber, and had commanded that nobody should have admittance to him. Concluding that he was immersed in sorrow for the death of her brother, and fearing to renew his tears by the sight of his sole remaining child, she hesitated

whether she should break in upon his affliction; yet solici-
tude for him, backed by the commands of her mother,
encouraged her to venture disobeying the orders he had
given; a fault she had never been guilty of before. The gentle
timidity of her nature made her pause for some minutes at
his door. She heard him traverse his chamber backwards
and forwards with disordered steps; a mood which increased her apprehensions. She was however just going to
beg admittance, when Manfred suddenly opened the door;
and as it was now twilight, concurring with the disorder of
his mind, he did not distinguish the person, but asked angrily who it was? Matilda replied trembling, My dearest
father, it is I, your daughter. Manfred, stepping back hastily,
cried, Begone, I do not want a daughter; and, flinging back
abruptly, clapped the door against the terrified Matilda.

She was too well acquainted with her father's impetuosity
to venture a second intrusion. When she had a little recovered the shock of so bitter a reception, she wiped away her
tears, to prevent the additional stab that the knowledge of it
would give to Hippolita, who questioned her in the most
anxious terms on the health of Manfred, and how he bore
his loss. Matilda assured her he was well, and supported his
misfortune with manly fortitude. But will he not let me see
him? said Hippolita mournfully: Will he not permit me to
blend my tears with his, and shed a mother's sorrows in the
bosom of her lord? Or do you deceive me, Matilda? I know
how Manfred doted on his son: Is not the stroke too heavy
for him? Has he not sunk under it?—You do not answer
me—Alas, I dread the worst!—Raise me, my maidens: I
will, I will see my lord. Bear me to him instantly; he is
dearer to me even than my children. Matilda made signs to
Isabella to prevent Hippolita's rising; and both these lovely
young women were using their gentle violence to stop and
calm the princess, when a servant on the part of Manfred
arrived, and told Isabella that his lord demanded to speak
with her.

With me! cried Isabella. Go, said Hippolita, relieved by a message from her lord: Manfred cannot support the sight of his own family. He thinks you less disordered than we are, and dreads the shock of my grief. Console him, dear Isabella, and tell him I will smother my own anguish rather than add to his.

It was now evening; the servant who conducted Isabella bore a torch before her. When they came to Manfred, who was walking impatiently about the gallery, he started and said hastily, Take away that light, and begone. Then shutting the door impetuously, he flung himself upon a bench against the wall, and bade Isabella sit by him. She obeyed trembling. I sent for you, lady, said he,—and then stopped under great appearance of confusion. My lord!—Yes, I sent for you on a matter of great moment, resumed he:—Dry your tears, young lady—you have lost your bridegroom:— yes, cruel fate, and I have lost the hopes of my race!—But Conrad was not worthy of your beauty.—How! my lord, said Isabella; sure you do not suspect me of not feeling the concern I ought? My duty and affection would have always—Think no more of him, interrupted Manfred; he was a sickly puny child, and heaven has perhaps taken him away that I might not trust the honours of my house on so frail a foundation. The line of Manfred calls for numerous supports. My foolish fondness for that boy blinded the eyes of my prudence—but it is better as it is. I hope in a few years to have reason to rejoice at the death of Conrad.

Words cannot paint the astonishment of Isabella. At first she apprehended that grief had disordered Manfred's understanding. Her next thought suggested that this strange discourse was designed to ensnare her: she feared that Manfred had perceived her indifference for his son: and in consequence of that idea she replied, Good my lord, do not doubt my tenderness; my heart would have accompanied my hand. Conrad would have engrossed all my care; and wherever fate shall dispose of me, I shall always cherish his memory, and regard your highness and the virtuous Hippolita as my parents. Curse on Hippolita! cried Manfred: forget her from this moment, as I do. In short, lady, you have missed a husband undeserving of your charms: they shall now be better disposed of. Instead of a sickly boy, you shall have a husband in the prime of his age, who will know how to value your beauties, and who may expect a numerous offspring. Alas, my lord, said Isabella, my mind is too sadly engrossed by the recent catastrophe in your family to think of another marriage. If ever my father returns, and it shall be his pleasure, I shall obey, as I did when I consented to give my hand to your son: but until his return permit me to remain under your hospitable roof, and employ the melancholy hours in assuaging yours, Hippolita's, and the fair Matilda's affliction.

I desired you once before, said Manfred angrily, not to name that woman; from this hour she must be a stranger to you, as she must be to me:—in short, Isabella, since I cannot give you my son, I offer you myself.—Heavens! cried Isabella, waking from her delusion, what do I hear! You, my lord! You! My father in law! the father of Conrad! the husband of the virtuous and tender Hippolita!—I tell you, said Manfred imperiously, Hippolita is no longer my wife; I divorce her from this hour. Too long has she cursed me by her unfruitfulness: my fate depends on having sons,—and this night I trust will give a new date to my hopes. At those words he seized the cold hand of Isabella, who was half-dead with fright and horror. She shrieked, and started from him. Manfred rose to pursue her; when the moon, which was now up, and gleamed in at the opposite casement, presented to his sight the plumes of the fatal helmet, which rose to the height of the windows, waving backwards and forwards in a tempestuous manner, and accompanied with a hollow and rustling sound. Isabella, who gathered courage from her situation, and who dreaded nothing so much as Manfred's pursuit of his declaration, cried, Look, my lord!

see heaven itself declares against your impious intentions!—
Heaven nor hell shall impede my designs, said Manfred,
advancing again to seize the princess. At that instant the
portrait of his grandfather, which hung over the bench
where they had been sitting, uttered a deep sigh and heaved
its breast.* Isabella, whose back was turned to the picture,
saw not the motion, nor knew whence the sound came, but
started and said, Hark my lord! what sound was that? and at
the same time made towards the door. Manfred, distracted
between the flight of Isabella, who had now reached the
stairs, and his inability to keep his eyes from the picture,
which began to move, had however advanced some steps
after her, still looking backwards on the portrait, when he
saw it quit its pannel, and descend on the floor with a grave
and melancholy air. Do I dream? cried Manfred returning,
or are the devils themselves in league against me? Speak,
infernal spectre! Or, if thou art my grandsire, why dost
thou too conspire against thy wretched descendant, who
too dearly pays for—Ere he could finish the sentence the
vision sighed again, and made a sign to Manfred to follow
him. Lead on! cried Manfred; I will follow thee to the gulph
of perdition.* The spectre marched sedately, but dejected,
to the end of the gallery, and turned into a chamber on the
right hand. Manfred accompanied him at a little distance,
full of anxiety and horror, but resolved. As he would have
entered the chamber, the door was clapped-to with violence
by an invisible hand. The prince, collecting courage from
this delay, would have forcibly burst open the door with his
foot, but found that it resisted his utmost efforts. Since hell
will not satisfy my curiosity, said Manfred, I will use the
human means in my power for preserving my race; Isabella
shall not escape me.

That lady, whose resolution had given way to terror the
moment she had quitted Manfred, continued her flight to
the bottom of the principal staircase. There she stopped, not
knowing whither to direct her steps, nor how to escape

from the impetuosity of the prince. The gates of the castle she knew were locked, and guards placed in the court. Should she, as her heart prompted her, go and prepare Hippolita for the cruel destiny that awaited her, she did not doubt but Manfred would seek her there, and that his violence would incite him to double the injury he meditated, without leaving room for them to avoid the impetuosity of his passions. Delay might give him time to reflect on the horrid measures he had conceived, or produce some circumstance in her favour, if she could for that night at least avoid his odious purpose.—Yet where conceal herself! How avoid the pursuit he would infallibly make throughout the castle! As these thoughts passed rapidly through her mind, she recollected a subterraneous passage* which led from the vaults of the castle to the church of saint Nicholas. Could she reach the altar before she was overtaken, she knew even Manfred's violence would not dare to profane the sacredness of the place; and she determined, if no other means of deliverance offered, to shut herself up for ever among the holy virgins, whose convent was contiguous to the cathedral. In this resolution, she seized a lamp that burned at the foot of the staircase, and hurried towards the secret passage.

The lower part of the castle was hollowed into several intricate cloisters; and it was not easy for one under so much anxiety to find the door that opened into the cavern. An awful silence reigned thoughout those subterraneous regions, except now and then some blasts of wind that shook the doors she had passd, and which grating on the rusty hinges were re-echoed through that long labyrinth of darkness. Every murmur struck her with new terror;—yet more she dreaded to hear the wrathful voice of Manfred urging his domestics to pursue her. She trod as softly as impatience would give her leave,—yet frequently stopped and listened to hear if she was followed. In one of those moments she thought she heard a sigh. She shuddered, and recoiled a few paces. In a moment she thought she heard the step of some person. Her blood curdled; she concluded it was Manfred. Every suggestion that horror could inspire rushed into her mind. She condemned her rash flight, which had thus exposed her to his rage in a place where her cries were not likely to draw any body to her assistance.—Yet the sound seemed not to come from behind;—if Manfred knew where she was, he must have followed her: she was still in one of the cloisters, and the steps she had heard were too distinct to proceed from the way she had come. Cheered with this reflection, and hoping to find a friend in whoever was not the prince; she was going to advance, when a door that stood a-jar, at some distance to the left, was opened gently; but ere her lamp, which she held up, could discover who opened it, the person retreated precipitately on seeing the light.

Isabella, whom every incident was sufficient to dismay, hesitated whether she should proceed. Her dread of Manfred soon outweighed every other terror. The very circumstance of the person avoiding her, gave her a sort of courage. It could only be, she thought, some domestic belonging to the castle. Her gentleness had never raised her an enemy, and conscious innocence made her hope that, unless sent by the prince's order to seek her, his servants would rather assist than prevent her flight. Fortifying herself with these reflections, and believing, by what she could observe, that she was near the mouth of the subterraneous cavern, she approached the door that had been opened; but a sudden gust of wind that met her at the door extinguished her lamp, and left her in total darkness.

Words cannot paint the horror of the princess's situation. Alone in so dismal a place, her mind imprinted with all the terrible events of the day, hopeless of escaping, expecting every moment the arrival of Manfred, and far from tranquil on knowing she was within reach of somebody, she knew not whom, who for some cause seemed concealed thereabouts, all these thoughts crowded on her distracted mind, and she was ready to sink under her apprehensions. She addressed herself to every saint in heaven, and inwardly implored their assistance. For a considerable time she remained in an agony of despair. At last, as softly as was possible, she felt for the door, and, having found it, entered trembling into the vault from whence she had heard the sigh and steps. It gave her a kind of momentary joy to perceive an imperfect ray of clouded moonshine gleam from the roof of the vault, which seemed to be fallen in, and from whence hung a fragment of earth or building, she could not distinguish which, that appeared to have been crushed inwards. She advanced eagerly towards this chasm, when she discerned a human form standing close against the wall.

She shrieked, believing it the ghost of her betrothed Conrad. The figure advancing, said in a submissive voice, Be not alarmed, lady; I will not injure you. Isabella, a little encouraged by the words and tone of voice of the stranger, and recollecting that this must be the person who had opened the door, recovered her spirits enough to reply, Sir, whoever you are, take pity on a wretched princess standing on the brink of destruction: assist me to escape from this fatal castle, or in a few moments I may be made miserable for ever. Alas! said the stranger, what can I do to assist you? I will die in your defence; but I am unacquainted with the castle, and want—Oh! said Isabella, hastily interrupting him, help me but to find a trap-door that must be hereabout, and it is the greatest service you can do me; for I have not a minute to lose. Saying these words she felt about on the pavement, and directed the stranger to search likewise for a smooth piece of brass inclosed in one of the stones. That, said she, is the lock, which opens with a spring, of which I know the secret. If I can find that, I may escape—if not, alas, courteous stranger, I fear I shall have involved you in my misfortunes: Manfred will suspect you for the accomplice of my flight, and you will fall a victim to his resentment. I

value not my life, said the stranger; and it will be some
comfort to lose it in trying to deliver you from his tyranny.
Generous youth, said Isabella, how shall I ever requite—As
she uttered those words, a ray of moonshine streaming
through a cranny of the ruin above shone directly on the
lock they sought—Oh, transport! said Isabella, here is the
trap-door! and taking out a key, she touched the spring,
which starting aside discovered an iron ring. Lift up the
door, said the princess. The stranger obeyed; and beneath
appeared some stone steps descending into a vault totally
dark. We must go down here, said Isabella: follow me; dark
and dismal as it is, we cannot miss our way; it leads directly
to the church of saint Nicholas—But perhaps, added the
princess modestly, you have no reason to leave the castle,
nor have I farther occasion for your service; in a few minutes I shall be safe from Manfred's rage—only let me know
to whom I am so much obliged. I will never quit you, said
the stranger eagerly, till I have placed you in safety—nor
think me, princess, more generous than I am: though you
are my principal care—The stranger was interrupted by a
sudden noise of voices that seemed approaching, and they
soon distinguished these words: Talk not to me of necro-
mancers; I tell you she must be in the castle; I will find her
in spite of enchantment.—Oh, heavens! cried Isabella, it is
the voice of Manfred! Make haste, or we are ruined! and
shut the trap-door after you. Saying this, she descended the
steps precipitately; and as the stranger hastened to follow
her, he let the door slip out of his hands: it fell, and the
spring closed over it. He tried in vain to open it, not having
observed Isabella's method of touching the spring, nor had
he many moments to make an essay.* The noise of the
falling door had been heard by Manfred, who, directed by
the sound, hastened thither, attended by his servants with
torches. It must be Isabella, cried Manfred before he entered
the vault; she is escaping by the subterraneous passage, but
she cannot have got far.—What was the astonishment of the

prince, when, instead of Isabella, the light of the torches discovered to him the young peasant, whom he thought confined under the fatal helmet! Traitor! said Manfred, how camest thou here! I thought thee in durance above in the court. I am no traitor, replied the young man boldly, nor am I answerable for your thoughts. Presumptuous villain! cried Manfred, dost thou provoke my wrath? Tell me; how hast thou escaped from above? Thou hast corrupted thy guards, and their lives shall answer it. My poverty, said the peasant calmly, will disculpate* them: though the ministers of a tyrant's wrath, to thee they are faithful, and but too willing to execute the orders which you unjustly imposed upon them. Art thou so hardy as to dare my vengeance? said the prince—but tortures shall force the truth from thee. Tell me, I will know thy accomplices. There was my accomplice! said the youth smiling, and pointing to the roof. Manfred ordered the torches to be held up, and perceived that one of the cheeks of the enchanted casque had forced its way through the pavement of the court, as his servants had let it fall over the peasant, and had broken through into the vault, leaving a gap through which the peasant had pressed himself some minutes before he was found by Isabella. Was that the way by which thou didst descend? said Manfred. It was, said the youth. But what noise was that, said Manfred, which I heard as I entered the cloister? A door clapped, said the peasant: I heard it as well as you. What door? said Manfred hastily. I am not acquainted with your castle, said the peasant; this is the first time I ever entered it, and this vault the only part of it within which I ever was. But I tell thee, said Manfred, [wishing to find out if the youth had discovered the trap-door] it was this way I heard the noise: my servants heard it too.—My lord, interrupted one of them officiously, to be sure it was the trap-door, and he was going to make his escape. Peace! blockhead,* said the prince angrily; if he was going to escape, how should he come on this side? I will know from his own mouth what noise it was

I heard. Tell me truly; thy life depends on thy veracity. My veracity is dearer to me than my life, said the peasant; nor would I purchase the one by forfeiting the other. Indeed! young philosopher! said Manfred contemptuously: tell me then, what was the noise I heard? Ask me what I can answer, said he, and put me to death instantly if I tell you a lie. Manfred, growing impatient at the steady valour and indifference of the youth, cried, Well then, thou man of truth! answer; was it the fall of the trap-door that I heard? It was, said the youth. It was! said the prince; and how didst thou come to know there was a trap-door here? I saw the plate of brass by a gleam of moonshine, replied he. But what told thee it was a lock? said Manfred: How didst thou discover the secret of opening it? Providence, that delivered me from the helmet, was able to direct me to the spring of a lock, said he. Providence should have gone a little farther, and have placed thee out of the reach of my resentment, said Manfred: when Providence had taught thee to open the lock, it abandoned thee for a fool, who did not know how to make use of its favours. Why didst thou not pursue the path pointed out for thy escape? Why didst thou shut the trap-door before thou hadst descended the steps? I might ask you, my lord, said the peasant, how I, totally unacquainted with your castle, was to know that those steps led to any outlet? but I scorn to evade your questions. Wherever those steps lead to, perhaps I should have explored the way—I could not have been in a worse situation than I was. But the truth is, I let the trap-door fall: your immediate arrival followed. I had given the alarm—what imported it to me whether I was seized a minute sooner or a minute later? Thou art a resolute villain for thy years, said Manfred—yet on reflection I suspect thou dost but trifle with me: thou hast not yet told me how thou didst open the lock. That I will show you, my lord, said the peasant; and taking up a fragment of stone that had fallen from above, he laid himself on the trap-door, and began to beat on the piece of brass that covered it; meaning to gain time for the escape of the princess. This presence of mind, joined to the frankness of the youth, staggered Manfred. He even felt a disposition towards pardoning one who had been guilty of no crime. Manfred was not one of those savage tyrants who wanton in cruelty unprovoked. The circumstances of his fortune had given an asperity to his temper, which was naturally humane; and his virtues were always ready to operate, when his passion did not obscure his reason.

While the prince was in this suspense, a confused noise of voices echoed through the distant vaults. As the sound approached, he distinguished the clamour of some of his domestics, whom he had dispersed through the castle in search of Isabella, calling out, Where is my lord? Where is the prince? Here I am, said Manfred, as they came nearer; have you found the princess? The first that arrived replied, Oh, my lord! I am glad we have found you.—Found me! said Manfred: have you found the princess? We thought we had, my lord, said the fellow looking terrified—but—But what? cried the prince: has she escaped?—Jaquez and I, my lord—Yes, I and Diego, interrupted the second, who came up in still greater consternation—Speak one of you at a time, said Manfred; I ask you, where is the princess? We do not know, said they both together: but we are frightened out of our wits.—So I think, blockheads, said Manfred: what is it has scared you thus?—Oh, my lord! said Jaquez, Diego has seen such a sight! your highness would not believe our eyes.—What new absurdity is this? cried Manfred—Give me a direct answer, or by heaven—Why, my lord, if it please your highness to hear me, said the poor fellow; Diego and I—Yes, I and Jaquez, cried his comrade—Did not I forbid you to speak both at a time? said the prince: You, Jaquez, answer; for the other fool seems more distracted than thou art; what is the matter? My gracious lord, said Jaquez, if it please your highness to hear me; Diego and I, according to your highness's orders, went to search for the young lady; but being comprehensive* that we might meet the ghost of my young lord, your highness's son, God rest his soul, as he has not received christian burial—Sot! cried Manfred in a rage, is it only a ghost then that thou hast seen? Oh, worse! worse! my lord! cried Diego: I had rather have seen ten whole ghosts.—Grant me patience! said Manfred; these blockheads distract me—Out of my sight, Diego! And thou, Jaquez, tell me in one word, art thou sober? art thou raving? Thou wast wont to have some sense: has the other sot frightened himself and thee too? Speak; what is it he fancies he has seen? Why, my lord, replied Jaquez trembling, I was going to tell you highness, that since the calamitous misfortune of my young lord, God rest his soul! not one of us your highness's faithful servants, indeed we are, my lord, though poor men; I say, not one of us has dared to set a foot about the castle, but two together: so Diego and I, thinking that my young lady might be in the great gallery, went up there to look for her, and tell her your highness wanted something to impart to her.—O blundering fools! cried Manfred: and in the mean time she has made her escape, because you were afraid of goblins! Why, thou knave! she left me in the gallery; I came from thence myself.—For all that, she may be there still for aught I know, said Jaquez; but the devil shall have me before I seek her there again!—Poor Diego! I do not believe he will ever recover it! Recover what? said Manfred; am I never to learn what it is has terrified these rascals? But I lose my time; follow me, slave! I will see if she is in the gallery.—For heaven's sake, my dear good lord, cried Jaquez, do not go to the gallery! Satan himself I believe is in the great chamber next to the gallery.—Manfred, who hitherto had treated the terror of his servants as an idle panic, was struck at this new circumstance. He recollected the apparition of the portrait, and the sudden closing of the door at the end of the gallery—his voice faltered, and he asked with disorder, what is in the great chamber? My lord, said Jaquez, when Diego and

I came into the gallery, he went first, for he said he had more courage than I. So when we came into the gallery, we found nobody. We looked under every bench and stool; and still we found nobody.—Were all the pictures in their places? said Manfred. Yes, my lord, answered Jaquez; but we did not think of looking behind them.—Well, well! said Manfred; proceed. When we came to the door of the great chamber, continued Jaquez, we found it shut.—And could not you open it? said Manfred. Oh! yes, my lord, would to heaven we had not! replied he—Nay, it was not I neither, it was Diego: he was grown foolhardy, and would go on, though I advised him not—If ever I open a door that is shut again—Trifle not, said Manfred shuddering, but tell me what you saw in the great chamber on opening the door.— I! my lord! said Jaquez, I saw nothing; I was behind Diego;—but I heard the noise.—Jaquez, said Manfred in a solemn tone of voice, tell me, I adjure thee by the souls of my ancestors, what it was thou sawest; what it was thou heardest. It was Diego saw it, my lord, it was not I, replied Jaquez; I only heard the noise. Diego had no sooner opened the door, than he cried out and ran back—I ran back too, and said, Is it the ghost? The ghost! No, no, said Diego, and his hair stood on end—it is a giant, I believe; he is all clad in armour, for I saw his foot and part of his leg,* and they are as large as the helmet below in the court. As he said these words, my lord, we heard a violent motion and the rattling of armour, as if the giant was rising; for Diego has told me since, that he believes the giant was lying down, for the foot and leg were stretched at length on the floor. Before we could get to the end of the gallery, we heard the door of the great chamber clap behind us, but we did not dare turn back to see if the giant was following us—Yet now I think on it, we must have heard him if he had pursued us—But for heaven's sake, good my lord, send for the chaplain and have the castle exorcised, for, for certain, it is enchanted. Ay, pray do, my lord, cried all the servants at once, or we must leave your highness's service.—Peace, dotards! said Manfred, and follow me; I will know what all this means. We! my lord! cried they with one voice; we would not go up to the gallery for your highness's revenue. The young peasant, who had stood silent, now spoke. Will your highness, said he, permit me to try this adventure? My life is of consequence to nobody: I fear no bad angel, and have offended no good one. Your behaviour is above your seeming, said Manfred; viewing him with surprise and admiration—hereafter I will reward your bravery—but now, continued he with a sigh, I am so circumstanced, that I dare trust no eyes but my own—However, I give you leave to accompany me.

Manfred, when he first followed Isabella from the gallery, had gone directly to the apartment of his wife, concluding the princess had retired thither. Hippolita, who knew his step, rose with anxious fondness to meet her lord, whom she had not seen since the death of their son. She would have flown in a transport mixed of joy and grief to his bosom; but he pushed her rudely off, and said, Where is Isabella? Isabella! my lord! said the astonished Hippolita. Yes, Isabella; cried Manfred imperiously; I want Isabella. My lord, replied Matilda, who perceived how much his behaviour had shocked her mother, she has not been with us since your highness summoned her to your apartment. Tell me where she is, said the prince; I do not want to know where she has been. My good lord, said Hippolita, your daughter tells you the truth: Isabella left us by your command, and has not returned since:—but, my good lord, compose yourself: retire to your rest: this dismal day has disordered you. Isabella shall wait your orders in the morning. What, then you know where she is? cried Manfred: tell me directly, for I will not lose an instant—And you, woman, speaking to his wife, order your chaplain to attend me forthwith. Isabella, said Hippolita calmly, is retired I suppose to her chamber: she is not accustomed to watch at this late hour. Gracious

my lord, continued she, let me know what has disturbed
you: has Isabella offended you? Trouble me not with questions, said Manfred, but tell me where she is. Matilda shall
call her, said the princess—sit down, my lord, and resume
your wonted fortitude.—What, art thou jealous of Isabella,
replied he, that you wish to be present at our interview?
Good heavens! my lord, said Hippolita, what is it your
highness means? Thou wilt know ere many minutes are
passed, said the cruel prince. Send your chaplain to me, and
wait my pleasure here. At these words he flung out of
the room in search of Isabella; leaving the amazed ladies
thunder-struck with his words and frantic deportment,
and lost in vain conjectures on what he was meditating.

Manfred was now returning from the vault, attended by
the peasant and a few of his servants whom he had obliged
to accompany him. He ascended the stair-case without
stopping till he arrived at the gallery, at the door of which he
met Hippolita and her chaplain. When Diego had been
dismissed by Manfred, he had gone directly to the princess's
apartment with the alarm of what he had seen. That excellent lady, who no more than Manfred doubted of the reality
of the vision, yet affected to treat it as a delirium of the
servant. Willing, however, to save her lord from any additional shock, and prepared by a series of grief not to tremble
at any accession to it; she determined to make herself the
first sacrifice, if fate had marked the present hour for their
destruction. Dismissing the reluctant Matilda to her rest,
who in vain sued for leave to accompany her mother, and
attended only by her chaplain, Hippolita had visited the
gallery and great chamber: and now, with more serenity of
soul than she had felt for many hours, she met her lord, and
assued him that the vision of the gigantic leg and foot was all
a fable; and no doubt an impression made by fear, and the
dark and dismal hour of the night, on the minds of his
servants: She and the chaplain had examined the chamber,
and found every thing in the usual order.

Manfred, though persuaded, like his wife, that the vision had been no work of fancy, recovered a little from the tempest of mind into which so many strange events had thrown him. Ashamed too of his inhuman treatment of a princess, who returned every injury with new marks of tenderness and duty, he felt returning love forcing itself into his eyes—but not less ashamed of feeling remorse towards one, against whom he was inwardly meditating a yet more bitter outrage, he curbed the yearnings of his heart, and did not dare to lean even towards pity. The next transition of his soul was to exquisite villainy. Presuming on the unshaken submission of Hippolita, he flattered himself that she would not only acquiesce with patience to a divorce, but would obey, if it was his pleasure, in endeavouring to persuade Isabella to give him her hand—But ere he could indulge this horrid hope, he reflected that Isabella was not to be found. Coming to himself, he gave orders that every avenue to the castle should be strictly guarded, and charged his domestics on pain of their lives to suffer nobody to pass out. The young peasant, to whom he spoke favourably, he ordered to remain in a small chamber on the stairs, in which there was a pallet-bed,* and the key of which he took away himself, telling the youth he would talk with him in the morning. Then dismissing his attendants, and bestowing a sullen kind of half-nod on Hippolita, he retired to his own chamber.

# CHAPTER II

MATILDA, who by Hippolita's order had retired to her apartment, was ill-disposed to take any rest. The shocking fate of her brother had deeply affected her. She was surprised at not seeing Isabella: but the strange words which had fallen from her father, and his obscure menace to the princess his wife, accompanied by the most furious behaviour, had filled her gentle mind with terror and alarm. She waited anxiously for the return of Bianca, a young damsel that attended her, whom she had sent to learn what was become of Isabella. Bianca soon appeared, and informed her mistress of what she had gathered from the servants, that Isabella was no where to be found. She related the adventure of the young peasant, who had been discovered in the vault, though with many simple additions from the incoherent accounts of the domestics; and she dwelled principally on the gigantic leg and foot which had been seen in the gallery-chamber. This last circumstance had terrified Bianca so much, that she was rejoiced when Matilda told her that she would not go to rest, but would watch till the princess should rise.

The young princess wearied herself in conjectures on the flight of Isabella, and on the threats of Manfred to her mother. But what business could he have so urgent with the chaplain? said Matilda. Does he intend to have my brother's body interred privately in the chapel? Oh! madam, said Bianca, now I guess. As you are become his heiress, he is impatient to have you married: he has always been raving for more sons; I warrant he is now impatient for grandsons. As sure as I live, madam, I shall see you a bride at last. Good madam, you won't cast off your faithful Bianca: you won't put Donna Rosara over me, now you are a great princess? My poor Bianca, said Matilda, how fast your thoughts amble! I a great princess! What hast thou seen in Manfred's behaviour since my brother's death that bespeaks any increase of tenderness to me? No, Bianca, his heart was ever a stranger to me—but he is my father, and I must not complain. Nay, if heaven shuts my father's heart against me, it over-pays my little merit in the tenderness of my mother— O that dear mother! Yes, Bianca, 'tis there I feel the rugged temper of Manfred. I can support his harshness to me with patience; but it wounds my soul when I am witness to his causeless severity towards her. Oh, madam, said Bianca, all men use their wives so, when they are weary of them.—And yet you congratulated me but now, said Matilda, when you fancied my father intended to dispose of me. I would have you a great lady, replied Bianca, come what will. I do not wish to see you moped in a convent, as you would be if you had your will, and if my lady your mother, who knows that a bad husband is better than no husband at all, did not hinder you.—Bless me! what noise is that? Saint Nicholas forgive me! I was but in jest. It is the wind, said Matilda, whistling through the battlements in the tower above: you have heard it a thousand times. Nay, said Bianca, there was no harm neither in what I said: it is no sin to talk of matrimony—And so, madam, as I was saying; if my lord Manfred should offer you a handsome young prince for a bridegroom, you would drop him a curtsy, and tell him you would rather take the veil. Thank heaven! I am in no such danger, said Matilda: you know how many proposals for me he has rejected.—And you thank him, like a dutiful daughter, do you, madam?—But come, madam; suppose, tomorrow morning he was to send for you to the great council-chamber, and there you should find at his elbow a lovely young prince, with large black eyes, a smooth white forehead, and manly curling locks like jet; in short, madam, a young hero resembling the picture of the good Alfonso in the gallery, which you sit and gaze at for hours together.— Do not speak lightly of that picture, interrupted Matilda sighing: I know the adoration with which I look at that picture is uncommon—but I am not in love with a coloured pannel. The character of that virtuous prince, the veneration with which my mother has inspired me for his memory, the orisons* which I know not why she has enjoined me to pour forth at his tomb, all have concurred to persuade me that somehow or other my destiny is linked with something relating to him.—Lord! madam, how should that be? said Bianca: I have always heard that your family was no way related to his: and I am sure I cannot conceive why my lady, the princess, sends you in a cold morning, or a damp evening, to pray at his tomb: he is no saint by the almanack. If you must pray, why does not she bid you address yourself to our great saint Nicholas? I am sure he is the saint I pray to for a husband. Perhaps my mind would be less affected, said Matilda, if my mother would explain her reasons to me: but it is the mystery she observes, that inspires me with this—I know not what to call it. As she never acts from caprice, I am sure there is some fatal secret at bottom—nay, I know there is: in her agony of grief for my brother's death she dropped some words that intimated as much.—Oh, dear madam, cried Bianca, what were they? No, said Matilda: if a parent lets fall a word, and wishes it recalled, it is not for a child to utter it. What! was she sorry for what she had said? asked Bianca —I am sure, madam, you may trust me.—With my own little secrets, when I have any, I may, said Matilda; but never with my mother's: a child ought to have no ears or eyes but as a parent directs. Well! to be sure, madam, you was born to be a saint, said Bianca, and there's no resisting one's vocation: you will end in a convent at last. But there is my lady Isabella would not be so reserved to me: she will let me talk to her of young men; and when a handsome cavalier has come to the castle, she has owned to me that she wished your brother Conrad resembled him. Bianca, said the princess, I do not allow you to mention my friend disrespectfully. Isabella is of a cheerful disposition, but her soul is pure as virtue itself. She knows your idle babbling humour, and perhaps has now and then encouraged it, to divert melancholy, and to enliven the solitude in which my father keeps us.—Blessed Mary! said Bianca starting, there it is again!—Dear madam, do you hear nothing?—This castle is certainly haunted!—Peace! said Matilda, and listen! I did think I heard a voice—but it must be fancy; your terrors I suppose have infected me. Indeed! indeed! madam, said Bianca, half-weeping with agony, I am sure I heard a voice. Does any body lie in the chamber beneath? said the princess. Nobody has dared to lie there, answered Bianca, since the great astrologer that was your brother's tutor drowned himself. For certain, madam, his ghost and the young prince's are now met in the chamber below—for heaven's sake let us fly to your mother's apartment! I charge you not to stir, said Matilda. If they are spirits in pain, we may ease their sufferings by questioning them.* They can mean no hurt to us, for we have not injured them—and if they should, shall we be more safe in one chamber than in another? Reach me my beads; we will say a prayer, and then speak to them. Oh, dear lady, I would not speak to a ghost for the world, cried Bianca—As she said those words, they heard the casement of the little chamber below Matilda's open. They listened attentively, and in few minutes thought they heard a person sing, but could not distinguish the words. This can be no evil spirit, said the princess in a low voice: it is undoubtedly one of the family—open the window, and we shall know the voice. I dare not indeed, madam, said Bianca. Thou art a very fool, said Matilda, opening the window gently herself. The noise the princess made was however heard by the person beneath, who stopped, and, they concluded, had heard the casement open. Is any body below? said the princess: if there is, speak. Yes, said an unknown voice. Who is it? said Matilda. A stranger, replied the voice. What stranger? said she; and how didst thou come there at this unusual hour, when all

the gates of the castle are locked? I am not here willingly,
answered the voice—but pardon me, lady, if I have disturbed your rest: I knew not that I was overheard. Sleep had
forsaken me: I left a restless couch, and came to waste the
irksome hours with gazing on the fair approach of morning,
impatient to be dismissed from this castle. Thy words and
accents, said Matilda, are of a melancholy cast: if thou art
unhappy, I pity thee. If poverty afflicts thee, let me know it;
I will mention thee to the princess, whose beneficent soul
ever melts for the distressed; and she will relieve thee. I am
indeed unhappy, said the stranger; and I know not what
wealth is: but I do not complain of the lot which heaven has
cast for me: I am young and healthy, and am not ashamed of
owing my support to myself—yet think me not proud, or
that I disdain your generous offers. I will remember you in
my orisons, and will pray for blessings on your gracious self
and your noble mistress—If I sigh, lady, it is for others, not
for myself. Now I have it, madam, said Bianca whispering
the princess. This is certainly the young peasant; and by my
conscience he is in love!—Well, this is a charming adventure!—Do, madam, let us sift* him. He does not know you,
but takes you for one of my lady Hippolita's women. Art
thou not ashamed, Bianca? said the princess: what right
have we to pry into the secrets of this young man's heart?
He seems virtuous and frank, and tells us he is unhappy: are
those circumstances that authorize us to make a property of
him? How are we entitled to his confidence? Lord! madam,
how little you know of love! replied Bianca: why, lovers
have no pleasure equal to talking of their mistress. And
would you have *me* become a peasant's confidante? said the
princess. Well then, let me talk to him, said Bianca: though
I have the honour of being your highness's maid of honour,
I was not always so great: besides, if love levels ranks, it
raises them too: I have a respect for any young man in
love.—Peace, simpleton! said the princess. Though he said
he was unhappy, it does not follow that he must be in love.

Think of all that has happened today, and tell me if there are no misfortunes but what love causes. Stranger, resumed the princess, if thy misfortunes have not been occasioned by thy own fault, and are within the compass of the princess Hippolita's power to redress, I will take upon me to answer that she will be thy protectress. When thou art dismissed from this castle, repair to holy father Jerome at the convent adjoining the church of saint Nicholas, and make thy story known to him, as far as thou thinkest meet: he will not fail to inform the princess, who is the mother of all that want her assistance. Farewell: it is not seemly for me to hold farther converse with a man at this unwonted hour. May the saints guard thee, gracious lady! replied the peasant—but oh, if a poor and worthless stranger might presume to beg a minute's audience farther—am I so happy?—the casement is not shut—might I venture to ask—Speak quickly, said Matilda; the morning dawns apace:* should the labourers come into the fields and perceive us—What wouldst thou ask—I know not how—I know not if I dare, said the young stranger faltering—yet the humanity with which you have spoken to me emboldens—Lady! dare I trust you?—Heavens! said Matilda, what dost thou mean? with what wouldst thou trust me? Speak boldly, if thy secret is fit to be entrusted to a virtuous breast.—I would ask, said the peasant, recollecting himself, whether what I have heard from the domestics is true, that the princess is missing from the castle? What imports it to thee to know? replied Matilda. Thy first words bespoke a prudent and becoming gravity. Dost thou come hither to pry into the secrets of Manfred? Adieu. I have been mistaken in thee.—Saying these words, she shut the casement hastily, without giving the young man time to reply. I had acted more wisely, said the princess to Bianca with some sharpness, if I had let thee converse with this peasant: his inquisitiveness seems of a piece with thy own. It is not fit for me to argue with your highness, replied Bianca; but perhaps the questions I should have put to him, would have been more to the purpose, than those you have been pleased to ask him. Oh, no doubt, said Matilda; you are a very discreet personage! May I know what you would have asked him? A by-stander often sees more of the game than those that play, answered Bianca. Does your highness think, madam, that his question about my lady Isabella was the result of mere curiosity? No, no, madam; there is more in it than you great folks are aware of. Lopez told me, that all the servants believe this young fellow contrived my lady Isabella's escape—Now, pray, madam, observe——You and I both know that my lady Isabella never much fancied the prince your brother.—Well! he is killed just in the critical minute—I accuse nobody. A helmet falls from the moon—so my lord your father says; but Lopez and all the servants say that this young spark* is a magician, and stole it from Alfonso's tomb.—Have done with this rhapsody of impertinence, said Matilda. Nay, madam, as you please, cried Bianca—yet it is very particular though, that my lady Isabella should be missing the very same day, and that this young sorcerer should be found at the mouth of the trap-door—I accuse nobody—but if my young lord came honestly by his death—Dare not on thy duty, said Matilda, to breathe a suspicion on the purity of my dear Isabella's fame.—Purity, or not purity, said Bianca, gone she is: a stranger is found that nobody knows; you question him yourself: he tells you he is in love, or unhappy, it is the same thing—nay, he owned he was unhappy about others; and is any body unhappy about another, unless they are in love with them? And at the very next word he asks innocently, poor soul! if my lady Isabella is missing.—To be sure, said Matilda, thy observations are not totally without foundation—Isabella's flight amazes me: the curiosity of this stranger is very particular—yet Isabella never concealed a thought from me.—So she told you, said Bianca, to fish out your secrets—but who knows, madam, but this stranger may be some prince in disguise?—Do, madam, let me open the window, and ask him a few questions. No, replied Matilda, I will ask him myself, if he knows aught of Isabella: he is not worthy that I should converse farther with him. She was going to open the casement, when they heard the bell ring at the postern-gate* of the castle, which is on the right hand of the tower, where Matilda lay. This prevented the princess from renewing the conversation with the stranger.

After continuing silent for some time; I am persuaded, said she to Bianca, that whatever be the cause of Isabella's flight, it had no unworthy motive. If this stranger was accessary to it, she must be satisfied of his fidelity and worth. I observed, did not you, Bianca? that his words were tinctured with an uncommon infusion of piety. It was no ruffian's speech: his phrases were becoming a man of gentle birth. I told you, madam, said Bianca, that I was sure he was some prince in disguise.—Yet, said Matilda, if he was privy to her escape, how will you account for his not accompanying her in her flight? Why expose himself unnecessarily and rashly to my father's resentment? As for that, madam, replied she, if he could get from under the helmet, he will find ways of eluding your father's anger. I do not doubt but he has some talisman or other about him.—You resolve every thing into magic, said Matilda—but a man who has any intercourse with infernal spirits does not dare to make use of those tremendous and holy words which he uttered. Didst thou not observe with what fervour he vowed to remember *me* to heaven in his prayers? Yes, Isabella was undoubtedly convinced of his piety.—Commend me to the piety of a young fellow and a damsel that consult to elope! said Bianca. No, no, madam; my lady Isabella is of another-guess mould* than you take her for. She used indeed to sigh and lift up her eyes in your company, because she knows you are a saint—but when your back was turned—You wrong her, said Matilda; Isabella is no hypocrite: she has a due sense of devotion, but never affected a call she has not.

On the contrary, she always combated my inclination for the cloister: and though I own the mystery she has made to me of her flight confounds me; though it seems inconsistent with the friendship between us; I cannot forget the disinterested warmth with which she always opposed my taking the veil: she wished to see me married, though my dower would have been a loss to her and my brother's children. For her sake I will believe well of this young peasant. Then you do think there is some liking between them? said Bianca.— While she was speaking, a servant came hastily into the chamber, and told the princess that the lady Isabella was found. Where? said Matilda. She has taken sanctuary in saint Nicholas's church, replied the servant: father Jerome has brought the news himself: he is below with his highness. Where is my mother? said Matilda. She is in her own chamber, madam, and has asked for you.

Manfred had risen at the first dawn of light, and gone to Hippolita's apartment, to enquire if she knew ought of Isabella. While he was questioning her, word was brought that Jerome demanded to speak with him. Manfred, little suspecting the cause of the friar's arrival, and knowing he was employed by Hippolita in her charities, ordered him to be admitted, intending to leave them together, while he pursued his search after Isabella. Is your business with me or the princess? said Manfred. With both, replied the holy man. The lady Isabella—What of her? interrupted Manfred eagerly—is at saint Nicholas's altar, replied Jerome. That is no business of Hippolita, said Manfred with confusion: let us retire to my chamber, father; and inform me how she came thither. No, my lord, replied the good man with an air of firmness and authority that daunted even the resolute Manfred, who could not help revering the saint-like virtues of Jerome: my commission is to both; and, with your highness's good-liking,* in the presence of both I shall deliver it—But first, my lord, I must interrogate the princess, whether she is acquainted with the cause of the lady

Isabella's retirement from your castle.—No, on my soul, said Hippolita; does Isabella charge me with being privy to it?—Father, interrupted Manfred, I pay due reverence to your holy profession; but I am sovereign here, and will allow no meddling priest to interfere in the affairs of my domestic. If you have aught to say, attend me to my chamber—I do not use to let my wife be acquainted with the secret affairs of my state; they are not within a woman's province. My lord, said the holy man, I am no intruder into the secrets of families. My office is to promote peace, to heal divisions, to preach repentance, and teach mankind to curb their headstrong passions. I forgive your highness's uncharitable apostrophe: I know my duty, and am the minister of a mightier prince than Manfred. Hearken to him who speaks through my organs. Manfred trembled with rage and shame. Hippolita's countenance declared her astonishment, and impatience to know where this would end: her silence more strongly spoke her observance of Manfred.

The lady Isabella, resumed Jerome, commends herself to both your highnesses; she thanks both for the kindness with which she has been treated in your castle: she deplores the loss of your son, and her own misfortune in not becoming the daughter of such wise and noble princes, whom she shall always respect as *parents*: she prays for uninterrupted union and felicity between you: [Manfred's colour changed]* but as it is no longer possible for her to be allied to you, she entreats your consent to remain in sanctuary till she can learn news of her father; or, by the certainty of his death, be at liberty, with the approbation of her guardians, to dispose of herself in suitable marriage. I shall give no such consent, said the prince; but insist on her return to the castle without delay: I am answerable for her person to her guardians, and will not brook her being in any hands but my own. Your highness will recollect whether that can any longer be proper, replied the friar. I want no monitor, said Manfred colouring. Isabella's conduct leaves room for strange suspicions—and that young villain, who was at least the accomplice of her flight, if not the cause of it—The cause! interrupted Jerome: was a *young* man the cause? This is not to be borne! cried Manfred. Am I to be bearded in my own palace by an insolent monk? Thou art privy, I guess, to their amours. I would pray to heaven to clear up your uncharitable surmises, said Jerome, if your highness were not satisfied in your conscience how unjustly you accuse me. I do pray to heaven to pardon that uncharitableness: and I implore your highness to leave the princess at peace in that holy place, where she is not liable to be disturbed by such vain and worldly fantasies as discourses of love from any man. Cant* not to me, said Manfred, but return, and bring the princess to her duty. It is my duty to prevent her return hither, said Jerome. She is where orphans and virgins are safest from the snares and wiles of this world; and nothing but a parent's authority shall take her thence. I am her parent, cried Manfred, and demand her. She wished to have you for her parent, said the friar; but heaven, that forbad that connexion, has for ever dissolved all ties betwixt you: and I announce to your highness—Stop! audacious man, said Manfred, and dread my displeasure. Holy father, said Hippolita, it is your office to be no respecter of persons: you must speak as your duty prescribes: but it is my duty to hear nothing that it pleases not my lord I should hear. I will retire to my oratory, and pray to the blessed Virgin to inspire you with her holy counsels, and to restore the heart of my gracious lord to its wonted peace and gentleness. Excellent woman! said the friar.—My lord, I attend your pleasure.

Manfred, accompanied by the friar, passed to his own apartment; where shutting the door, I perceive, father, said he, that Isabella has acquainted you with my purpose. Now hear my resolve, and obey. Reasons of state, most urgent reasons, my own and the safety of my people, demand that I should have a son. It is in vain to expect an heir from

Hippolita. I have made choice of Isabella. You must bring her back; and you must do more. I know the influence you have with Hippolita: her conscience is in your hands. She is, I allow, a faultless woman: her soul is set on heaven, and scorns the little grandeur of this world: you can withdraw her from it entirely. Persuade her to consent to the dissolution of our marriage, and to retire into a monastery—she shall endow one if she will; and she shall have the means of being as liberal to your order as she or you can wish. Thus you will divert the calamities that are hanging over our heads, and have the merit of saving the principality of Otranto from destruction. You are a prudent man; and though the warmth of my temper betrayed me into some unbecoming expressions, I honour your virtue, and wish to be indebted to you for the repose of my life and the preservation of my family.

The will of heaven be done! said the friar. I am but its worthless instrument. It makes use of my tongue to tell thee, prince, of thy unwarrantable designs. The injuries of the virtuous Hippolita have mounted to the throne of pity. By me thou art reprimanded for thy adulterous intention of repudiating her: by me thou art warned not to pursue the incestuous design on thy contracted daughter. Heaven, that delivered her from thy fury, when the judgments so recently fallen on thy house ought to have inspired thee with other thoughts, will continue to watch over her. Even I, a poor and despised friar, am able to protect her from thy violence.—I, sinner as I am, and uncharitably reviled by your highness as an accomplice of I know not what amours, scorn the allurements with which it has pleased thee to tempt mine honesty. I love my order; I honour devout souls; I respect the piety of thy princess—but I will not betray the confidence she reposes in me, nor serve even the cause of religion by foul and sinful compliances—But forsooth! the welfare of the state depends on your highness having a son. Heaven mocks the short-sighted views of man. But yester-morn, whose house was so great, so flourishing as Manfred's?—Where is young Conrad now?—My lord, I respect your tears—but I mean not to check them—Let them flow, prince! they will weigh more with heaven towards the welfare of thy subjects, than a marriage, which, founded on lust or policy, could never prosper. The sceptre, which passed from the race of Alfonso to thine, cannot be preserved by a match which the church will never allow. If it is the will of the Most High that Manfred's name must perish, resign yourself, my lord, to its decrees; and thus deserve a crown that can never pass away.—Come, my lord, I like this sorrow—Let us return to the princess: she is not apprized of your cruel intentions; nor did I mean more than to alarm you. You saw with what gentle patience, with what efforts of love, she heard, she rejected hearing the extent of your guilt. I know she longs to fold you in her arms, and assure you of her unalterable affection. Father, said the prince, you mistake my compunction: true, I honour Hippolita's virtues; I think her a saint; and wish it were for my soul's health to tie faster the knot that has united us.—But alas! father, you know not the bitterest of my pangs! It is some time that I have had scruples on the legality of our union: Hippolita is related to me in the fourth degree*—It is true, we had a dispensation; but I have been informed that she had also been contracted to another. This it is that sits heavy at my heart: to this state of unlawful wedlock I impute the visitation that has fallen on me in the death of Conrad!—Ease my conscience of this burden; dissolve our marriage, and accomplish the work of godliness which your divine exhortations have commenced in my soul.

How cutting was the anguish which the good man felt, when he perceived this turn in the wily prince! He trembled for Hippolita, whose ruin he saw was determined; and he feared, if Manfred had no hope of recovering Isabella, that his impatience for a son would direct him to some other object, who might not be equally proof against the temptation of Manfred's rank. For some time the holy man remained absorbed in thought. At length, conceiving some hope from delay, he thought the wisest conduct would be to prevent the prince from despairing of recovering Isabella. Her the friar knew he could dispose, from her affection to Hippolita, and from the aversion she had expressed to him for Manfred's addresses, to second his views, till the censures of the church could be fulminated* against a divorce. With this intention, as if struck with the prince's scruples, he at length said, My lord, I have been pondering on what your highness has said; and if in truth it is delicacy of conscience that is the real motive of your repugnance to your virtuous lady, far be it from me to endeavour to harden your heart! The church is an indulgent mother; unfold your griefs to her: she alone can administer comfort to your soul, either by satisfying your conscience, or, upon examination of your scruples, by setting you at liberty, and indulging you in the lawful means of continuing your lineage. In the latter case, if the lady Isabella can be brought to consent——Manfred, who concluded that he had either over-reached the good man, or that his first warmth had been but a tribute paid to appearance, was overjoyed at this sudden turn, and repeated the most magnificent promises, if he should succeed by the friar's mediation. The well-meaning priest suffered him to deceive himself, fully determined to traverse his views,* instead of seconding them.

Since we now understand one another, resumed the prince, I expect, father, that you satisfy me in one point. Who is the youth that we found in the vault? He must have been privy to Isabella's flight: tell me truly; is he her lover? or is he an agent for another's passion? I have often suspected Isabella's indifference to my son: a thousand circumstances crowd on my mind that confirm that suspicion. She herself was so conscious of it, that, while I discoursed her in the gallery, she outran my suspicions, and endeavoured to justify herself from coolness to Conrad. The friar, who knew nothing of the youth but what he had learnt occasionally from the princess, ignorant what was become of him, and not sufficiently reflecting on the impetuosity of Manfred's temper, conceived that it might not be amiss to sow the seeds of jealousy in his mind: they might be turned to some use hereafter, either by prejudicing the prince against Isabella, if he persisted in that union; or, by diverting his attention to a wrong scent, and employing his thoughts on a visionary intrigue, prevent his engaging in any new pursuit. With this unhappy policy, he answered in a manner to confirm Manfred in the belief of some connexion between Isabella and the youth. The prince, whose passions wanted little fuel to throw them into a blaze, fell into a rage at the idea of what the friar suggested. I will fathom to the bottom of this intrigue, cried he; and quitting Jerome abruptly, with a command to remain there till his return, he hastened to the great hall of the castle, and ordered the peasant to be brought before him.

Thou hardened young impostor! said the prince, as soon as he saw the youth; what becomes of thy boasted veracity now? It was Providence, was it, and the light of the moon, that discovered the lock of the trap-door to thee? Tell me, audacious boy, who thou art, and how long thou hast been acquainted with the princess— and take care to answer with less equivocation that thou didst last night, or tortures shall wring the truth from thee. The young man, perceiving that his share in the flight of the princess was discovered, and concluding that any thing he should say could no longer be of service or detriment to her, replied, I am no impostor, my lord; nor have I deserved opprobrious language. I answered to every question your highness put to me last night with the same veracity that I shall speak now: and that will not be from fear of your tortures, but because my soul abhors a falsehood. Please to repeat your questions, my lord; I am ready to give you all the satisfaction in my power. You

know my questions, replied the prince, and only want time
to prepare an evasion. Speak directly; who art thou? and
how long hast thou been known to the princess? I am a
labourer at the next village, said the peasant; my name is
Theodore. The princess found me in the vault last night:
before that hour I never was in her presence.—I may believe
as much or as little as I please of this, said Manfred; but I
will hear thy own story, before I examine into the truth of
it. Tell me, what reason did the princess give thee for making her escape? Thy life depends on thy answer. She told
me, replied Theodore, that she was on the brink of destruction; and that, if she could not escape from the castle, she
was in danger in a few moments of being made miserable for
ever. And on this slight foundation, on a silly girl's report,
said Manfred, thou didst hazard my displeasure? I fear no
man's displeasure, said Theodore, when a woman in distress
puts herself under my protection.—During this examination, Matilda was going to the apartment of Hippolita. At
the upper end of the hall, where Manfred sat, was a
boarded* gallery with latticed windows, through which
Matilda and Bianca were to pass. Hearing her father's
voice, and seeing the servants assembled round him, she
stopped to learn the occasion. The prisoner soon drew her
attention: the steady and composed manner in which he
answered, and the gallantry of his last reply, which were
the first words she heard distinctly, interested her in his
favour. His person was noble, handsome and commanding,
even in that situation: but his countenance soon engrossed
her whole care. Heavens! Bianca, said the princess softly, do
I dream? or is not that youth the exact resemblance of
Alfonso's picture in the gallery? She could say no more, for
her father's voice grew louder at every word. This bravado,
said he, surpasses all thy former insolence. Thou shalt
experience the wrath with which thou darest to trifle. Seize
him, continued Manfred, and bind him—the first news the
princess hears of her champion shall be, that he has lost his

head for her sake. The injustice of which thou art guilty towards me, said Theodore, convinces me that I have done a good deed in delivering the princess from thy tyranny. May she be happy, whatever becomes of me!—This is a lover! cried Manfred in a rage: a peasant within sight of death is not animated by such sentiments. Tell me, tell me, rash boy, who thou art, or the rack shall force thy secret from thee. Thou hast threatened me with death already, said the youth, for the truth I have told thee: if that is all the encouragement I am to expect for sincerity, I am not tempted to indulge thy vain curiosity farther. Then thou wilt not speak? said Manfred. I will not, replied he. Bear him away into the court-yard, said Manfred; I will see his head this instant severed from his body.—Matilda fainted at hearing those words. Bianca shrieked, and cried, Help! help! the princess is dead! Manfred started at this ejaculation, and demanded what was the matter. The young peasant, who heard it too, was struck with horror, and asked eagerly the same question; but Manfred ordered him to be hurried into the court, and kept there for execution, till he had informed himself of the cause of Bianca's shrieks. When he learned the meaning, he treated it as a womanish panic; and ordering Matilda to be carried to her apartment, he rushed into the court, and, calling for one of his guards, bade Theodore kneel down and prepare to receive the fatal blow.

The undaunted youth received the bitter sentence with a resignation that touched every heart but Manfred's. He wished earnestly to know the meaning of the words he had heard relating to the princess; but, fearing to exasperate the tyrant more against her, he desisted. The only boon he deigned to ask was, that he might be permitted to have a confessor, and make his peace with heaven. Manfred, who hoped by the confessor's means to come at the youth's history, readily granted his request: and being convinced that father Jerome was now in his interest, he ordered him to be called and shrieve the prisoner. The holy man, who had little foreseen the catastrophe that his imprudence occasioned, fell on his knees to the prince, and adjured him in the most solemn manner not to shed innocent blood. He accused himself in the bitterest terms for his indiscretion, endeavoured to disculpate the youth, and left no method untried to soften the tyrant's rage. Manfred, more incensed than appeased by Jerome's intercession, whose retraction now made him suspect he had been imposed upon by both, commanded the friar to do his duty, telling him he would not allow the prisoner many minutes for confession. Nor do I ask many, my lord, said the unhappy young man. My sins, thank heaven! have not been numerous; nor exceed what might be expected at my years. Dry your tears, good father, and let us dispatch: this is a bad world; nor have I had cause to leave it with regret. Oh! wretched youth! said Jerome; how canst thou bear the sight of me with patience? I am thy murderer! It is I have brought this dismal hour upon thee!—I forgive thee from my soul, said the youth, as I hope heaven will pardon me. Hear my confession, father; and give me thy blessing. How can I prepare thee for thy passage, as I ought? said Jerome. Thou canst not be saved without pardoning thy foes—and canst thou forgive that impious man there? I can, said Theodore; I do.—And does not this touch thee, cruel prince? said the friar. I sent for thee to confess him, said Manfred sternly; not to plead for him. Thou didst first incense me against him—his blood be upon thy head!—It will! it will! said the good man in an agony of sorrow. Thou and I must never hope to go where this blessed youth is going.—Dispatch! said Manfred: I am no more to be moved by the whining of priests, than by the shrieks of women. What! said the youth, is it possible that my fate could have occasioned what I heard? Is the princess then again in thy power?—Thou dost but remember me of my wrath, said Manfred: prepare thee, for this moment is thy last. The youth, who felt his indignation rise, and who was touched with the sorrow which he saw he had infused into all the spectators, as well as into the friar, suppressed his emotions, and, putting off his doublet and unbuttoning his collar, knelt down to his prayers. As he stooped, his shirt flipped down below his shoulder, and discovered the mark of a bloody arrow.* Gracious heaven! cried the holy man starting, what do I see? It is my child! my Theodore!

The passions that ensued must be conceived; they cannot be painted. The tears of the assistants were suspended by wonder, rather than stopped by joy. They seemed to enquire in the eyes of their lord what they ought to feel. Surprise, doubt, tenderness, respect, succeeded each other in the countenance of the youth. He received with modest submission the effusion of the old man's tears and embraces: yet afraid of giving a loose to hope, and suspecting from what had passed the inflexibility of Manfred's temper, he cast a glance towards the prince, as if to say, Canst thou be unmoved at such a scene as this?

Manfred's heart was capable of being touched. He forgot his anger in his astonishment; yet his pride forbad his owning himself affected. He even doubted whether this discovery was not a contrivance of the friar to save the youth. What may this mean! said he. How can he be thy son? Is it consistent with thy profession or reputed sanctity to avow a peasant's offspring for the fruit of thy irregular amours?— Oh God! said the holy man, dost thou question his being mine? Could I feel the anguish I do, if I were not his father? Spare him! good prince, spare him! and revile me as thou pleasest.—Spare him! spare him! cried the attendants, for this good man's sake!—Peace! said Manfred sternly: I must know more, ere I am disposed to pardon. A saint's bastard may be no saint himself—Injurious lord! said Theodore: add not insult to cruelty. If I am this venerable man's son, though no prince as thou art, know, the blood that flows in my veins—Yes, said the friar, interrupting him, his blood is noble: nor is he that abject thing, my lord, you speak him.

He is my lawful son; and Sicily can boast of few houses more ancient than that of Falconara—But alas! my lord, what is blood? what is nobility? We are all reptiles, miserable sinful creatures. It is piety alone that can distinguish us from the dust whence we sprung, and whither we must return.—Truce to your sermon, said Manfred; you forget you are no longer friar Jerome, but the count of Falconara. Let me know your history; you will have time to moralize hereafter, if you should not happen to obtain the grace of that sturdy criminal there. Mother of God! said the friar, is it possible my lord can refuse a father the life of his only, his long lost child? Trample me, my lord, scorn, afflict me, accept my life for his, but spare my son!—Thou canst feel then, said Manfred, what it is to lose an only son? A little hour ago thou didst preach up resignation to me: *my* house, if fate so pleased, must perish—but the count of Falconara—Alas! my lord, said Jerome, I confess I have offended; but aggravate not an old man's sufferings. I boast not of my family, nor think of such vanities—it is nature that pleads for this boy; it is the memory of the dear woman that bore him—Is she, Theodore, is she dead?—Her soul has long been with the blessed, said Theodore. Oh how? cried Jerome, tell me—No—she is happy! Thou art all my care now!—Most dread lord! will you—will you grant me my poor boy's life? Return to thy convent, answered Manfred; conduct the princess hither; obey me in what else thou knowest; and I promise thee the life of thy son.——Oh! my lord, said Jerome, is honesty the price I must pay for this dear youth's safety?—For me! cried Theodore: let me die a thousand deaths, rather than stain thy conscience. What is it the tyrant would exact of thee? Is the princess safe from his power? Protect her, thou venerable old man! and let all his wrath fall on me. Jerome endeavoured to check the impetuosity of the youth; and ere Manfred could reply, the trampling of horses was heard, and a brazen* trumpet, which hung without the gate of the castle, was suddenly sounded. At the same instant the sable plumes on the enchanted helmet, which still remained at the other end of the court, were tempestuously agitated, and nodded thrice, as if bowed by some invisible wearer.

# CHAPTER III

MANFRED's heart misgave him when he beheld the plumage on the miraculous casque shaken in concert with the sounding of the brazen trumpet. Father! said he to Jerome, whom he now ceased to treat as count of Falconara, what mean these portents? If I have offended—[the plumes were shaken with greater violence than before] Unhappy prince that I am! cried Manfred—Holy Father! will you not assist me with your prayers?—My lord, replied Jerome, heaven is no doubt displeased with your mockery of its servants. Submit yourself to the church; and cease to persecute her ministers. Dismiss this innocent youth; and learn to respect the holy character I wear: heaven will not be trifled with: you see—[the trumpet sounded again] I acknowledge I have been too hasty, said Manfred. Father, do you go to the wicket, and demand who is at the gate. Do you grant me the life of Theodore? replied the friar. I do, said Manfred; but enquire who is without.

Jerome, falling on the neck of his son, discharged a flood of tears, that spoke the fulness of his soul. You promised to go to the gate, said Manfred. I thought, replied the friar, your highness would excuse my thanking you first in this tribute of my heart. Go, dearest sir, said Theodore, obey the prince; I do not deserve that you should delay his satisfaction for me.

Jerome, enquiring who was without, was answered, A herald. From whom? said he. From the knight of the gigantic sabre, said the herald: and I must speak with the usurper of Otranto. Jerome returned to the prince, and did not fail to repeat the message in the very words it had been uttered. The first sounds struck Manfred with terror; but when he heard himself styled usurper, his rage rekindled, and all his courage revived. Usurper!—Insolent villain! cried he, who

dares to question my title? Retire, father; this is no business
for monks: I will meet this presumptuous man myself. Go
to your convent, and prepare the princess's return: your son
shall be a hostage for your fidelity: his life depends on your
obedience.—Good heaven! my lord, cried Jerome, your
highness did but this instant freely pardon my child—have
you so soon forgot the interposition of heaven?—Heaven,
replied Manfred, does not send heralds to question the title
of a lawful prince—I doubt whether it even notifies its will
through friars—but that is your affair, not mine. At present
you know my pleasure; and it is not a saucy herald that shall
save your son, if you do not return with the princess.

It was in vain for the holy man to reply. Manfred commanded him to be conducted to the postern-gate, and shut
out from the castle: and he ordered some of his attendants to
carry Theodore to the top of the black tower, and guard him
strictly; scarce permitting the father and son to exchange a
hasty embrace at parting. He then withdrew to the hall, and,
seating himself in princely state, ordered the herald to be
admitted to his presence.

Well, thou insolent, said the prince, what wouldst thou
with me? I come, replied he, to thee, Manfred, usurper of
the principality of Otranto, from the renowned and invin-
cible knight, the knight of the gigantic sabre: in the name of
his lord, Frederic marquis of Vicenza, he demands the lady
Isabella, daughter of that prince, whom thou hast basely and
traitorously got into thy power, by bribing her false guardians during his absence: and he requires thee to resign the
principality of Otranto, which thou hast usurped from the
said lord Frederic, the nearest of blood to the last rightful
lord Alfonso the Good. If thou dost not instantly comply
with these just demands, he defies thee to single combat to
the last extremity. And so saying, the herald cast down his
warder.*

And where is this braggart, who sends thee? said
Manfred. At the distance of a league, said the herald: he

comes to make good his lord's claim against thee, as he is a true knight, and thou an usurper and ravisher.

Injurious as this challenge was, Manfred reflected that it was not his interest to provoke the marquis. He knew how well-founded the claim of Frederic was; nor was this the first time he had heard of it. Frederic's ancestors had assumed the style of princes of Otranto, from the death of Alfonso the Good without issue: but Manfred, his father, and grandfather, had been too powerful for the house of Vicenza to dispossess them. Frederic, a martial and amorous young prince, had married a beautiful young lady, of whom he was enamoured, and who had died in childbed of Isabella. Her death affected him so much, that he had taken the cross and gone to the Holy Land, where he was wounded in an engagement against the infidels, made prisoner, and reported to be dead. When the news reached Manfred's ears, he bribed the guardians of the lady Isabella to deliver her up to him as a bride for his son Conrad; by which alliance he had purposed to unite the claims of the two houses. This motive, on Conrad's death, had co-operated to make him so suddenly resolve on espousing her himself; and the same reflection determined him now to endeavour at obtaining the consent of Frederic to this marriage. A like policy inspired him with the thought of inviting Frederic's champion into his castle, lest he should be informed of Isabella's flight, which he strictly enjoined his domestics not to disclose to any of the knight's retinue.

Herald, said Manfred, as soon as he had digested these reflections, return to thy master, and tell him, ere we liquidate our differences by the sword, Manfred would hold some converse with him. Bid him welcome to my castle, where, by my faith, as I am a true knight, he shall have courteous reception, and full security for himself and followers. If we cannot adjust our quarrel by amicable means, I swear he shall depart in safety, and shall have full satisfaction according to the law of arms: so help me God and his holy Trinity!—The herald made three obeisances, and retired.

During this interview Jerome's mind was agitated by a thousand contrary passions. He trembled for the life of his son, and his first idea was to persuade Isabella to return to the castle. Yet he was scarce less alarmed at the thought of her union with Manfred. He dreaded Hippolita's unbounded submission to the will of her lord: and though he did not doubt but he could alarm her piety not to consent to a divorce, if he could get access to her; yet should Manfred discover that the obstruction came from him, it might be equally fatal to Theodore. He was impatient to know whence came the herald, who with so little management* had questioned the title of Manfred: yet he did not dare absent himself from the convent, lest Isabella should leave it, and her flight be imputed to him. He returned disconsolately to the monastery, uncertain on what conduct to resolve. A monk, who met him in the porch and observed his melancholy air, said, Alas! brother, is it then true that we have lost our excellent princess Hippolita? The holy man started, and cried, What meanest thou, brother? I come this instant from the castle, and left her in perfect health. Martelli, replied the other friar, passed by the convent but a quarter of an hour ago on his way from the castle, and reported that her highness was dead. All our brethren are gone to the chapel to pray for her happy transit to a better life, and willed me to wait thy arrival. They know thy holy attachment to that good lady, and are anxious for the affliction it will cause in thee—Indeed we have all reason to weep; she was a mother to our house—But this life is but a pilgrimage; we must not murmur—we shall all follow her; may our end be like hers!—Good brother, thou dreamest, said Jerome: I tell thee I come from the castle, and left the princess well—Where is the lady Isabella?—Poor gentlewoman! replied the friar; I told her the sad news, and offered her spiritual comfort; I reminded her of the transitory condition of mortality, and advised her to take the veil: I quoted the example of the holy princess Sanchia of Arragon.*—Thy zeal was laudable, said Jerome impatiently; but at present it was unnecessary: Hippolita is well—at least I trust in the Lord she is; I heard nothing to the contrary—Yet methinks the prince's earnestness—Well, brother, but where is the lady Isabella?—I know not, said the friar: she wept much, and said she would retire to her chamber. Jerome left his comrade abruptly, and hasted to the princess, but she was not in her chamber. He enquired of the domestics of the convent, but could learn no news of her. He searched in vain throughout the monastery and the church, and dispatched messengers round the neighbourhood, to get intelligence if she had been seen; but to no purpose. Nothing could equal the good man's perplexity. He judged that Isabella, suspecting Manfred of having precipitated his wife's death, had taken the alarm, and withdrawn herself to some more secret place of concealment. This new flight would probably carry the prince's fury to the height. The report of Hippolita's death, though it seemed almost incredible, increased his consternation; and though Isabella's escape bespoke her aversion of Manfred for a husband, Jerome could feel no comfort from it, while it endangered the life of his son. He determined to return to the castle, and made several of his brethren accompany him, to attest his innocence to Manfred, and, if necessary, join their intercession with his for Theodore.

The prince, in the mean time, had passed into the court, and ordered the gates of the castle to be flung open for the reception of the stranger knight and his train. In a few minutes the cavalcade arrived.* First came two harbingers* with wands. Next a herald, followed by two pages and two trumpets. Then an hundred foot-guards. These were attended by as many horse. After them fifty footmen, clothed in scarlet and black, the colours of the knight. Then a led horse. Two heralds on each side of a gentleman on horseback bearing a banner with the arms of Vicenza and Otranto quarterly*—a circumstance that much offended Manfred—but he stifled his resentment. Two more pages. The knight's confessor telling his beads. Fifty more footmen, clad as before. Two knights habited in complete armour, their beavers* down, comrades to the principal knight. The 'squires of the two knights, carrying their shields and devices. The knight's own 'squire. An hundred gentlemen bearing an enormous sword, and seeming to faint under the weight of it. The knight himself on a chestnut steed, in complete armour, his lance in the rest, his face entirely concealed by his vizor, which was surmounted by a large plume of scarlet and black feathers. Fifty foot-guards with drums and trumpets closed the procession, which wheeled off to the right and left to make room for the principal knight.

As soon as he approached the gate, he stopped; and the herald advancing, read again the words of the challenge. Manfred's eyes were fixed on the gigantic sword, and he scarce seemed to attend to the cartel:* but his attention was soon diverted by a tempest of wind that rose behind him. He turned, and beheld the plumes of the enchanted helmet agitated in the same extraordinary manner as before. It required intrepidity like Manfred's not to sink under a concurrence of circumstances that seemed to announce his fate. Yet scorning in the presence of strangers to betray the courage he had always manifested, he said boldly, Sir knight, whoever thou art, I bid thee welcome. If thou art of mortal mould, thy valour shall meet its equal: and if thou art a true knight, thou wilt scorn to employ sorcery to carry thy point. Be these omens from heaven or hell, Manfred trusts to the righteousness of his cause and to the aid of saint Nicholas, who has ever protected his house. Alight, sir knight, and repose thyself. To-morrow thou shalt have a fair field; and heaven befriend the juster side!

The knight made no reply, but, dismounting, was

conducted by Manfred to the great hall of the castle. As they traversed the court, the knight stopped to gaze at the miraculous casque; and, kneeling down, seemed to pray inwardly for some minutes. Rising, he made a sign to the prince to lead on. As soon as they entered the hall, Manfred proposed to the stranger to disarm; but the knight shook his head in token of refusal. Sir knight, said Manfred, this is not courteous; but by my good faith I will not cross thee! nor shalt thou have cause to complain of the prince of Otranto. No treachery is designed on my part: I hope none is intended on thine. Here take my gage:* [giving him his ring] your friends and you shall enjoy the laws of hospitality. Rest here until refreshments are brought: I will but give orders for the accommodation of your train, and return to you. The three knights bowed, as accepting his courtesy. Manfred directed the stranger's retinue to be conducted to an adjacent hospital,* founded by the princess Hippolita for the reception of pilgrims. As they made the circuit of the court to return towards the gate, the gigantic sword burst from the supporters, and, falling to the ground opposite to the helmet, remained immoveable. Manfred, almost hardened to preternatural appearances, surmounted the shock of this new prodigy; and returning to the hall, where by this time the feast was ready, he invited his silent guests to take their places. Manfred, however ill his heart was at ease, endeavoured to inspire the company with mirth. He put several questions to them, but was answered only by signs. They raised their vizors but sufficiently to feed themselves, and that sparingly. Sirs, said the prince, ye are the first guests I ever treated within these walls, who scorned to hold any intercourse with me: nor has it oft been customary, I ween, for princes to hazard their state and dignity against strangers and mutes. You say you come in the name of Frederic of Vicenza: I have ever heard that he was a gallant and courteous knight; nor would he, I am bold to say, think it beneath him to mix in social converse with a prince that is his equal, and not unknown by deeds in arms.—Still ye are silent—Well! be it as it may—by the laws of hospitality and chivalry ye are masters under this roof: ye shall do your pleasure—but come, give me a goblet of wine; ye will not refuse to pledge me to the healths of your fair mistresses. The principal knight sighed and crossed himself, and was rising from the board—Sir knight, said Manfred, what I said was but in sport: I shall constrain you in nothing; use your good liking. Since mirth is not your mood, let us be sad. Business may hit your fancies better: let us withdraw; and hear if what I have to unfold may be better relished than the vain efforts I have made for your pastime.

Manfred, then, conducting the three knights into an inner chamber, shut the door, and, inviting them to be seated, began thus, addressing himself to the chief personage:

You come, sir knight, as I understand, in the name of the marquis of Vicenza, to re-demand the lady Isabella his daughter, who has been contracted in the face of holy church to my son, by the consent of her legal guardians; and to require me to resign my dominions to your lord, who gives himself for the nearest of blood to prince Alfonso, whose soul God rest! I shall speak to the latter article of your demands first. You must know, your lord knows, that I enjoy the principality of Otranto from my father Don Manuel, as he received it from his father Don Ricardo. Alfonso, their predecessor, dying childless in the Holy Land, bequeathed his estates to my grandfather Don Ricardo, in consideration of his faithful services—[The stranger shook his head]—Sir knight, said Manfred warmly, Ricardo was a valiant and upright man; he was a pious man; witness his munificent foundation of the adjoining church and two convents. He was peculiarly patronized by saint Nicholas—My grandfather was incapable—I say, sir, Don Ricardo was incapable—Excuse me, your interruption has disordered me—I venerate the memory of my grand-father—Well, sirs! he held this estate; he held it by his good sword, and by the favour of saint Nicholas—so did my father; and so, sirs, will I, come what will.—But Frederic, your lord, is nearest in blood—I have consented to put my title to the issue of the sword—does that imply a vitious* title? I might have asked, where is Frederic, your lord? Report speaks him dead in captivity. You say, your actions say, he lives—I question it not—I might, sirs, I might—but I do not. Other princes would bid Frederic take his inheritance by force, if he can: they would not stake their dignity on a single combat: they would not submit it to the decision of unknown mutes! Pardon me, gentlemen, I am too warm: but suppose yourselves in my situation: as ye are stout knights, would it not move your choler to have your own and the honour of your ancestors called in question?—But to the point. Ye require me to deliver up the lady Isabella— Sirs, I must ask if ye are authorized to receive her? [The knight nodded.] Receive her—continued Manfred: Well! you are authorized to receive her—But, gentle knight, may I ask if you have full powers? [The knight nodded.] 'Tis well, said Manfred: then hear what I have to offer—Ye see, gentlemen, before you the most unhappy of men! [he began to weep] afford me your compassion; I am entitled to it; indeed I am. Know, I have lost my only hope, my joy, the support of my house—Conrad died yester-morning. [The knights discovered signs of surprise.] Yes, sirs, fate has disposed of my son. Isabella is at liberty.—Do you then restore her, cried the chief knight, breaking silence. Afford me your patience, said Manfred. I rejoice to find, by this testimony of your good-will, that this matter may be adjusted without blood. It is no interest of mine dictates what little I have farther to say. Ye behold in me a man disgusted with the world: the loss of my son has weaned me from earthly cares. Power and greatness have no longer any charms in my eyes. I wished to transmit the sceptre I had received from my ancestors with honour to my son—but that is over! Life itself is so indifferent to me, that I accepted your defiance with joy: a good knight cannot go to the grave with more satisfaction than when falling in his vocation. Whatever is the will of heaven, I submit; for, alas! sirs, I am a man of many sorrows. Manfred is no object of envy—but no doubt you are acquainted with my story. [The knight made signs of ignorance, and seemed curious to have Manfred proceed.] Is it possible, sirs, continued the prince, that my story should be a secret to you? Have you heard nothing relating to me and the princess Hippolita? [They shook their heads]—No! Thus then, sirs, it is. You think me ambitious: ambition, alas, is composed of more rugged materials. If I were ambitious, I should not for so many years have been a prey to the hell of conscientious scruples—But I weary your patience: I will be brief. Know then, that I have long been troubled in mind on my union with the princess Hippolita.—Oh! sirs, if ye were acquainted with that excellent woman! if ye knew that I adore her like a mistress, and cherish her as a friend—But man was not born for perfect happiness! She shares my scruples, and with her consent I have brought this matter before the church, for we are related within the forbidden degrees. I expect every hour the definitive sentence that must separate us forever. I am sure you feel for me—I see you do—Pardon these tears! [The knights gazed on each other, wondering where this would end.] Manfred continued: The death of my son betiding while my soul was under this anxiety, I thought of nothing but resigning my dominions, and retiring forever from the sight of mankind. My only difficulty was to fix on a successor, who would be tender of my people, and to dispose of the lady Isabella, who is dear to me as my own blood. I was willing to restore the line of Alfonso, even in his most distant kindred: and though, pardon me, I am satisfied it was his will that Ricardo's lineage should take place of his own relations; yet, where was I to search for those relations? I knew of none but Frederic, your lord: he was a captive to the infidels, or dead; and were he living, and at home, would he quit the flourishing state of Vicenza for the inconsiderable principality of Otranto? If he would not, could I bear the thought of seeing a hard unfeeling viceroy set over my poor faithful people?—for, sirs, I love my people, and thank heaven am beloved by them.—But ye will ask, Whither tends this long discourse? Briefly then, thus, sirs. Heaven in your arrival seems to point out a remedy for these difficulties and my misfortunes. The lady Isabella is at liberty: I shall soon be so. I would submit to any thing for the good of my people—Were it not the best, the only way to extinguish the feuds between our families, if I were to take the lady Isabella to wife?—You start—But though Hippolita's virtues will ever be dear to me, a prince must not consider himself; he is born for his people.—A servant at that instant entering the chamber, apprized Manfred that Jerome and several of his brethren demanded immediate access to him.

The prince, provoked at this interruption, and fearing that the friar would discover to the strangers that Isabella had taken sanctuary, was going to forbid Jerome's entrance. But recollecting that he was certainly arrived to notify the princess's return, Manfred began to excuse himself to the knights for leaving them for a few moments, but was prevented by the arrival of the friars. Manfred angrily reprimanded them for their intrusion, and would have forced them back from the chamber; but Jerome was too much agitated to be repulsed. He declared aloud the flight of Isabella, with protestations of his own innocence. Manfred, distracted at the news, and not less at its coming to the knowledge of the strangers, uttered nothing but incoherent sentences, now upbraiding the friar, now apologizing to the knights, earnest to know what was become of Isabella, yet equally afraid of their knowing, impatient to pursue her, yet dreading to have them join in the pursuit. He offered to dispatch messengers in quest of her:—but the chief knight, no longer keeping silence, reproached Manfred in bitter terms for his dark and ambiguous dealing, and demanded the cause of Isabella's first absence from the castle. Manfred, casting a stern look at Jerome, implying a command of silence, pretended that on Conrad's death he had placed her in sanctuary until he could determine how to dispose of her. Jerome, who trembled for his son's life, did not dare contradict this falsehood; but one of his brethren, not under the same anxiety, declared frankly that she had fled to their church in the preceding night. The prince in vain endeavoured to stop this discovery, which overwhelmed him with shame and confusion. The principal stranger, amazed at the contradictions he heard, and more than half persuaded that Manfred had secreted the princess, notwithstanding the concern he expressed at her flight, rushing to the door, said, Thou traitor-prince! Isabella shall be found. Manfred endeavoured to hold him; but the other knights assisting their comrade, he broke from the prince, and hastened into the court, demanding his attendants. Manfred, finding it in vain to divert him from the pursuit, offered to accompany him; and summoning his attendants, and taking Jerome and some of the friars to guide them, they issued from the castle; Manfred privately giving orders to have the knight's company secured, while to the knight he affected to dispatch a messenger to require their assistance.

The company had no sooner quitted the castle, than Matilda, who felt herself deeply interested for the young peasant, since she had seen him condemned to death in the hall, and whose thoughts had been taken up with concerting measures to save him, was informed by some of the female attendants that Manfred had dispatched all his men various ways in pursuit of Isabella. He had in his hurry given this order in general terms, not meaning to extend it to the guard he had set upon Theodore, but forgetting it. The domestics, officious to obey so peremptory a prince, and urged by their own curiosity and love of novelty to join in any precipitate chace, had to a man left the castle. Matilda disengaged herself from her women, stole up to the black tower, and, unbolting the door, presented herself to the astonished Theodore. Young man, said she, though filial duty and womanly modesty condemn the step I am taking, yet holy charity, surmounting all other ties, justifies this act. Fly; the doors of thy prison are open: my father and his domestics are absent; but they may soon return: begone in safety; and may the angels of heaven direct thy course!—Thou art surely one of those angels! said the enraptured Theodore: none but a blessed saint could speak, could act, could look like thee!—May I not know the name of my divine protectress? Methought thou namedst thy father: is it possible? can Manfred's blood feel holy pity?—Lovely lady, thou answerest not—But how art thou here thyself? Why dost thou neglect thy own safety, and waste a thought on a wretch like Theodore? Let us fly together: the life thou bestowest shall be dedicated to thy defence. Alas! thou mistakest, said Matilda sighing: I am Manfred's daughter, but no dangers await me. Amazement! said Theodore: but last night I blessed myself for yielding thee the service thy gracious compassion so charitably returns me now. Still thou art in an error, said the princess; but this is no time for explanation. Fly, virtuous youth, while it is in my power to save thee: should my father return, thou and I both should indeed have cause to tremble. How? said Theodore: thinkest thou, charming maid, that I will accept of life at the hazard of aught calamitous to thee? Better I endured a thousand deaths——I run no risk, said Matilda, but by thy delay. Depart: it cannot be known that I assisted thy flight. Swear by the saints above, said Theodore, that thou canst not be suspected; else here I vow to await whatever can befall me. Oh! thou art too generous, said Matilda; but rest assured that no suspicion can alight on me. Give me thy beauteous hand in token that thou dost not deceive me, said Theodore; and let me bathe it with the warm tears of gratitude.—Forbear, said the princess: this must not be.—Alas!

said Theodore, I have never known but calamity until this hour—perhaps shall never know other fortune again: suffer the chaste raptures of holy gratitude: 'tis my soul would print its effusions on thy hand.—Forbear, and begone, said Matilda: how would Isabella approve of seeing thee at my feet? Who is Isabella? said the young man with surprise. Ah me! I fear, said the princess, I am serving a deceitful one! Hast thou forgot thy curiosity this morning?—Thy looks, thy actions, all thy beauteous self seems an emanation of divinity, said Theodore, but thy words are dark and mysterious——Speak, lady, speak to thy servant's comprehension.—Thou understandest but too well, said Matilda: but once more I command thee to be gone: thy blood, which I may preserve, will be on my head, if I waste the time in vain discourse. I go, lady, said Theodore, because it is thy will, and because I would not bring the grey hairs of my father with sorrow to the grave. Say but, adored lady, that I have thy gentle pity.—Stay, said Matilda; I will conduct thee to the subterraneous vault by which Isabella escaped; it will lead thee to the church of saint Nicholas, where thou mayst take sanctuary.—What! said Theodore, was it another, and not thy lovely self, that I assisted to find the subterraneous passage? It was, said Matilda: but ask no more; I tremble to see thee still abide here: fly to the sanctuary.—To sanctuary! said Theodore: No princess; sanctuaries are for helpless damsels, or for criminals. Theodore's soul is free from guilt, nor will wear the appearance of it. Give me a sword, lady, and thy father shall learn that Theodore scorns an ignominious flight. Rash youth! said Matilda, thou wouldst not dare to lift thy presumptuous arm against the prince of Otranto? Not against *thy* father; indeed I dare not, said Theodore: excuse me, lady; I had forgotten—but could I gaze on thee, and remember thou art sprung from the tyrant Manfred?—But he is thy father, and from this moment my injuries are buried in oblivion. A deep and hollow groan, which seemed to come

from above, startled the princess and Theodore. Good
heaven! we are overheard! said the princess. They listened;
but perceiving no farther noise, they both concluded it the
effect of pent-up vapours:* and the princess, preceding
Theodore softly, carried him to her father's armoury; where
equipping him with a complete suit, he was conducted by
Matilda to the postern-gate. Avoid the town, said the princess, and all the western side of the castle: 'tis there the
search must be making by Manfred and the strangers: but
hie thee to the opposite quarter. Yonder, behind that forest
to the east is a chain of rocks, hollowed into a labyrinth of
caverns that reach to the sea-coast. There thou mayst lie
concealed, till thou canst make signs to some vessel to put
on shore and take thee off. Go! heaven be thy guide!—and
sometimes in thy prayers remember—Matilda!—Theodore
flung himself at her feet, and seizing her lily hand, which
with struggles she suffered him to kiss, he vowed on the
earliest opportunity to get himself knighted, and fervently
entreated her permission to swear himself eternally her
knight.—Ere the princess could reply, a clap of thunder was
suddenly heard, that shook the battlements. Theodore, regardless of the tempest, would have urged his suit; but the
princess, dismayed, retreated hastily into the castle, and
commanded the youth to be gone, with an air that would
not be disobeyed. He sighed, and retired, but with eyes
fixed on the gate, until Matilda closing it put an end to an
interview, in which the hearts of both had drunk so deeply
of a passion which both now tasted for the first time.

Theodore went pensively to the convent, to acquaint his
father with his deliverance. There he learned the absence of
Jerome, and the pursuit that was making after the lady
Isabella, with some particulars of whose story he now first
became acquainted. The generous gallantry of his nature
prompted him to wish to assist her; but the monks could
lend him no lights to guess at the route she had taken. He
was not tempted to wander far in search of her; for the idea

of Matilda had imprinted itself so strongly on his heart, that he could not bear to absent himself at much distance from her abode. The tenderness Jerome had expressed for him concurred to confirm this reluctance; and he even persuaded himself that filial affection was the chief cause of his hovering between the castle and monastery. Until Jerome should return at night, Theodore at length determined to repair to the forest that Matilda had pointed out to him. Arriving there, he sought the gloomiest shades, as best suited to the pleasing melancholy that reigned in his mind. In this mood he roved insensibly to the caves* which had formerly served as a retreat to hermits, and were now reported round the country to be haunted by evil spirits. He recollected to have heard this tradition; and being of a brave and adventurous disposition, he willingly indulged his curiosity in exploring the secret recesses of this labyrinth. He had not penetrated far before he thought he heard the steps of some person who seemed to retreat before him. Theodore, though firmly grounded in all our holy faith enjoins to be believed, had no apprehension that good men were abandoned without cause to the malice of the powers of darkness. He thought the place more likely to be infested by robbers, than by those infernal agents who are reported to molest and bewilder travellers. He had long burned with impatience to approve* his valour. Drawing his sabre, he marched sedately onwards, still directing his steps as the imperfect rustling sound before him led the way. The armour he wore was a like indication to the person who avoided him. Theodore, now convinced that he was not mistaken, redoubled his pace, and evidently gained on the person that fled; whose haste increasing, Theodore came up just as a woman fell breathless before him. He hasted to raise her; but her terror was so great, that he apprehended she would faint in his arms. He used every gentle word to dispel her alarms, and assured her that, far from injuring, he would defend her at the peril of his life. The lady recovering her spirits from his courteous demeanour, and gazing on her protector, said, Sure I have heard that voice before?—Not to my knowledge, replied Theodore, unless, as I conjecture, thou art the lady Isabella.—Merciful heaven! cried she, thou art not sent in quest of me, art thou? And saying those words she threw herself at his feet, and besought him not to deliver her up to Manfred. To Manfred! cried Theodore—No, lady: I have once already delivered thee from his tyranny, and it shall fare hard with me now, but I will place thee out of the reach of his daring. Is it possible, said she, that thou shouldst be the generous unknown I met last night in the vault of the castle? Sure thou art not a mortal, but my guardian angel: on my knees let me thank—Hold, gentle princess, said Theodore, nor demean thyself before a poor and friendless young man. If heaven has selected me for thy deliverer, it will accomplish its work, and strengthen my arm in thy cause. But come, lady, we are too near the mouth of the cavern; let us seek its inmost recesses: I can have no tranquillity till I have placed thee beyond the reach of danger.— Alas! what mean you, sir? said she. Though all your actions are noble, though your sentiments speak the purity of your soul, is it fitting that I should accompany you alone into these perplexed retreats? Should we be found together, what would a censorious world think of my conduct?*—I respect your virtuous delicacy, said Theodore; nor do you harbour a suspicion that wounds my honour. I meant to conduct you into the most private cavity of these rocks; and then, at the hazard of my life, to guard their entrance against every living thing. Besides, lady, continued he, drawing a deep sigh, beauteous and all perfect as your form is, and though my wishes are not guiltless of aspiring, know, my soul is dedicated to another; and although——A sudden noise prevented Theodore from proceeding. They soon distinguished these sounds, Isabella! What ho! Isabella!—The trembling princess relapsed into her former agony of fear. Theodore endeavoured to encourage her, but in vain. He assured her he would die rather than suffer her to return under Manfred's power; and begging her to remain concealed, he went forth to prevent the person in search of her from approaching.

At the mouth of the cavern he found an armed knight discoursing with a peasant, who assured him he had seen a lady enter the passes of the rock. The knight was preparing to seek her, when Theodore, placing himself in his way, with his sword drawn, sternly forbad him at his peril to advance. And who are thou who darest to cross my way? said the knight haughtily. One who does not dare more than he will perform, said Theodore. I seek the lady Isabella, said the knight; and understand she has taken refuge among these rocks. Impede me not, or thou wilt repent having provoked my resentment.—Thy purpose is as odious as thy resentment is contemptible, said Theodore. Return whence thou camest, or we shall soon know whose resentment is most terrible.—The stranger, who was the principal knight that had arrived from the marquis of Vicenza, had galloped from Manfred as he was busied in getting information of the princess, and giving various orders to prevent her falling into the power of the three knights. Their chief had suspected Manfred of being privy to the princess's absconding; and this insult from a man who he concluded was stationed by that prince to secrete her, confirming his suspicions, he made no reply, but, discharging a blow with his sabre at Theodore, would soon have removed all obstruction, if Theodore, who took him for one of Manfred's captains, and who had no sooner given the provocation than prepared to support it, had not received the stroke on his shield. The valour that had so long been smothered in his breast, broke forth at once: he rushed impetuously on the knight, whose pride and wrath were not less powerful incentives to hardy deeds. The combat was furious, but not long. Theodore wounded the knight in three several places, and at last disarmed him as he fainted by the loss of blood. The peasant, who had fled on the first onset, had given the alarm to some of Manfred's domestics, who by his orders were dispersed through the forest in pursuit of Isabella. They came up as the knight fell, whom they soon discovered to be the noble stranger. Theodore, notwithstanding his hatred to Manfred, could not behold the victory he had gained without emotions of pity and generosity: but he was more touched, when he learned the quality of his adversary, and was informed that he was no retainer, but an enemy of Manfred. He assisted the servants of the latter in disarming the knight, and in endeavouring to staunch the blood that flowed from his wounds. The knight, recovering his speech, said in a faint and faltering voice, Generous foe, we have both been in an error: I took thee for an instrument of the tyrant; I perceive thou hast made the like mistake—It is too late for excuses—I faint.—If Isabella is at hand, call her—I have important secrets to—He is dying! said one of the attendants; has nobody a crucifix about them? Andrea, do thou pray over him.—Fetch some water, said Theodore, and pour it down his throat, while I hasten to the princess. Saying this, he flew to Isabella; and in a few words told her modestly, that he had been so unfortunate by mistake as to wound a gentleman from her father's court, who wished ere he died to impart something of consequence to her. The princess, who had been transported at hearing the voice of Theodore as he called her to come forth, was astonished at what she heard. Suffering herself to be conducted by Theodore, the new proof of whose valour recalled her dispersed spirits, she came where the bleeding knight lay speechless on the ground—but her fears returned when she beheld the domestics of Manfred. She would again have fled, if Theodore had not made her observe that they were unarmed, and had not threatened them with instant death, if they should dare to seize the princess. The stranger, opening his eyes, and beholding a woman, said, Art thou—pray tell me truly—art thou Isabella of Vicenza? I am, said she; good heaven restore thee!—Then thou—then thou—said the knight, struggling for utterance—seest—thy father!—Give me one——Oh! amazement! horror! what do I hear? what do I see? cried Isabella. My father! You my father! How come you here, sir? For heaven's sake speak!—Oh! run for help, or he will expire!—'Tis most true, said the wounded knight, exerting all his force; I am Frederic thy father—Yes, I came to deliver thee—It will not be—Give me a parting kiss, and take——Sir, said Theodore, do not exhaust yourself: suffer us to convey you to the castle.—To the castle! said Isabella: Is there no help nearer than the castle? Would you expose my father to the tyrant? If he goes thither, I dare not accompany him.—And yet, can I leave him?—My child, said Frederic, it matters not for me whither I am carried: a few minutes will place me beyond danger: but while I have eyes to dote on thee, forsake me not, dear Isabella! This brave knight—I know not who he is—will protect thy innocence. Sir, you will not abandon my child, will you?— Theodore, shedding tears over his victim, and vowing to guard the princess at the expence of his life, persuaded Frederic to suffer himself to be conducted to the castle. They placed him on a horse belonging to one of the domestics, after binding up his wounds as well as they were able. Theodore marched by his side; and the afflicted Isabella, who could not bear to quit him, followed mournfully behind.

# CHAPTER IV

THE sorrowful troop no sooner arrived at the castle, than they were met by Hippolita and Matilda, whom Isabella had sent one of the domestics before to advertise of their approach. The ladies, causing Frederic to be conveyed into the nearest chamber, retired, while the surgeons examined his wounds. Matilda blushed at seeing Theodore and Isabella together; but endeavoured to conceal it by embracing the latter, and condoling with her on her father's mischance. The surgeons soon came to acquaint Hippolita that none of the marquis's wounds were dangerous; and that he was desirous of seeing his daughter and the princesses. Theodore, under pretence of expressing his joy at being freed from his apprehensions of the combat being fatal to Frederic, could not resist the impulse of following Matilda. Her eyes were so often cast down on meeting his, that Isabella, who regarded Theodore as attentively as he gazed on Matilda, soon divined who the object was that he had told her in the cave engaged his affections. While this mute scene passed, Hippolita demanded of Frederic the cause of his having taken that mysterious course for reclaiming his daughter; and threw in various apologies to excuse her lord for the match contracted between their children. Frederic, however incensed against Manfred, was not insensible to the courtesy and benevolence of Hippolita: but he was still more struck with the lovely form of Matilda. Wishing to detain them by his bedside, he informed Hippolita of his story. He told her, that, while prisoner to the infidels, he had dreamed that his daughter, of whom he had learned no news since his captivity, was detained in a castle, where she was in danger of the most dreadful misfortunes; and that if he obtained his liberty, and repaired to a wood near Joppa,* he would learn more. Alarmed at this dream, and incapable of obeying the direction given by it, his chains became more grievous than ever. But while his thoughts were occupied on the means of obtaining his liberty, he received the agreeable news that the confederate princes, who were warring in Palestine, had paid his ransom. He instantly set out for the wood that had been marked in his dream. For three days he and his attendants had wandered in the forest without seeing a human form: but on the evening of the third they came to a cell, in which they found a venerable hermit in the agonies of death. Applying rich cordials, they brought the saint-like man to his speech. My sons, said he, I am bounden to your charity—but it is in vain—I am going to my eternal rest—yet I die with the satisfaction of performing the will of heaven. When first I repaired to this solitude, after seeing my country become a prey to unbelievers [it is, alas! above fifty years since I was witness to that dreadful scene!] saint Nicholas appeared to me, and revealed a secret, which he bade me never disclose to mortal man, but on my death-bed. This is that tremendous hour, and ye are no doubt the chosen warriors to whom I was ordered to reveal my trust. As soon as ye have done the last offices to this wretched corse, dig under the seventh tree on the left hand of this poor cave, and your pains will—Oh! good heaven receive my soul! With those words the devout man breathed his last. By break of day, continued Frederic, when we had committed the holy relics to earth, we dug according to direction—But what was our astonishment, when about the depth of six feet we discovered an enormous sabre—the very weapon yonder in the court? On the blade, which was then partly out of the scabbard, though since closed by our efforts in removing it, were written the following lines—— No; excuse me, madam, added the marquis, turning to Hippolita, if I forbear to repeat them: I respect your sex and rank, and would not be guilty of offending your ear with sounds injurious to aught that is dear to you.—He paused. Hippolita trembled. She did not doubt but Frederic was destined by heaven to accomplish the fate that seemed to threaten her house. Looking with anxious fondness at Matilda, a silent tear stole down her cheek; but recollecting herself, she said, Proceed, my lord; heaven does nothing in vain: mortals must receive its divine behests with lowliness and submission. It is our part to deprecate its wrath, or bow to its decrees. Repeat the sentence, my lord: we listen resigned.—Frederic was grieved that he had proceeded so far. The dignity and patient firmness of Hippolita penetrated him with respect, and the tender silent affection, with which the princess and her daughter regarded each other, melted him almost to tears. Yet apprehensive that his forbearance to obey would be more alarming, he repeated in a faltering and low voice the following lines:

> Where'er a casque that suits this sword is found,
> With perils is thy daughter compass'd round:
> Alfonso's blood alone can save the maid,
> And quiet a long-restless prince's shade.

What is there in these lines, said Theodore impatiently, that affects these princesses? Why were they to be shocked by a mysterious delicacy, that has so little foundation? Your words are rude, young man, said the marquis; and though fortune has favoured you once—My honoured lord, said Isabella, who resented Theodore's warmth, which she perceived was dictated by his sentiments for Matilda, discompose not yourself for the glosing* of a peasant's son: he forgets the reverence he owes you; but he is not accustomed—Hippolita, concerned at the heat that had arisen, checked Theodore for his boldness, but with an air acknowledging his zeal; and, changing the conversation, demanded of Frederic where he had left her lord? As the marquis was going to reply, they heard a noise without; and rising to enquire the cause, Manfred; Jerome, and part of the troop, who had met an imperfect rumour of what had happened, entered the chamber. Manfred advanced hastily towards Frederic's bed to condole with him on his misfortune, and to learn the circumstances of the combat; when starting in an agony of terror and amazement, he cried, Ha! what art thou, thou dreadful spectre! Is my hour come?—My dearest, gracious lord, cried Hippolita, clasping him in her arms, what is it you see? Why do you fix your eye-balls thus?*—What! cried Manfred breathless—dost thou see nothing; Hippolita? Is this ghastly phantom sent to me alone—to me, who did not——For mercy's sweetest self, my lord, said Hippolita, resume your soul, command your reason. There is none here but we, your friends.—What, is not that Alfonso? cried Manfred: dost thou not see him? Can it be my brain's delirium?—This! my lord, said Hippolita: this is Theodore, the youth who has been so unfortunate—Theodore! said Manfred mournfully, and striking his forehead—Theodore, or a phantom, he has unhinged the soul of Manfred.—But how comes he here! and how comes he in armour? I believe he went in search of Isabella, said Hippolita. Of Isabella? said Manfred, relapsing into rage—Yes, yes, that is not doubtful—But how did he escape from durance in which I left him? Was it Isabella, or this hypocritical old friar, that procured his enlargement?—And would a parent be criminal, my lord, said Theodore, if he meditated the deliverance of his child? Jerome, amazed to hear himself in a manner accused by his son, and without foundation, knew not what to think. He could not comprehend how Theodore had escaped, how he came to be armed, and to encounter Frederic. Still he would not venture to ask any questions that might tend to inflame Manfred's wrath against his son. Jerome's silence convinced Manfred that he had contrived Theodore's release.—And is it thus, thou ungrateful old man, said the prince, addressing himself to the friar, that thou repayest mine and Hippolita's bounties? And not content with traversing my heart's nearest wishes, thou armest thy bastard, and bringest him into my own castle to insult me!—My lord, said Theodore, you wrong my father, nor he nor I is capable of harbouring a thought against your peace. Is it insolence thus to surrender myself to your highness's pleasure? added he, laying his sword respectfully at Manfred's feet. Behold my bosom; strike, my lord, if you suspect that a disloyal thought is lodged there. There is not a sentiment engraven on my heart, that does not venerate you and yours. The grace and fervour with which Theodore uttered these words, interested every person present in his favour. Even Manfred was touched—yet still possessed with his resemblance to Alfonso, his admiration was dashed with secret horror. Rise, said he; thy life is not my present purpose.—But tell me thy history, and how thou camest connected with this old traitor here. My lord! said Jerome eagerly.—Peace, impostor! said Manfred; I will not have him prompted. My lord, said Theodore, I want no assistance; my story is very brief. I was carried at five years of age to Algiers with my mother, who had been taken by corsairs from the coast of Sicily.* She died of grief in less than a twelvemonth.—The tears gushed from Jerome's eyes, on whose countenance a thousand anxious passions stood expressed. Before she died, continued Theodore, she bound a writing about my arm under my garments, which told me I was the son of the count Falconara.—It is most true, said Jerome; I am that wretched father.—Again I enjoin thee silence, said Manfred: proceed. I remained in slavery, said Theodore, until within these two years, when attending on my master in his cruizes, I was delivered by a christian vessel, which over-powered the pirate; and discovering myself to the captain, he generously put me on shore in Sicily. But alas! instead of finding a father, I learned that his estate, which was situated on the coast, had during his absence been laid waste by the rover who had carried my mother and me into captivity: that his castle had been burnt to the ground: and that my father on his return had sold what remained, and was retired into religion in the kingdom of Naples, but where, no man could inform me. Destitute and friendless, hopeless almost of attaining the transport of a parent's embrace, I took the first opportunity of setting sail for Naples; from whence within these six days I wandered into this province, still supporting myself by the labour of my hands; nor till yester-morn did I believe that heaven had reserved any lot for me but peace of mind and contented poverty. This, my lord, is Theodore's story. I am blessed beyond my hope in finding a father; I am unfortunate beyond my desert in having incurred your highness's displeasure. He ceased. A murmur of approbation gently arose from the audience. This is not all, said Frederic; I am bound in honour to add what he suppresses. Though he is modest, I must be gener-ous—he is one of the bravest youths on christian ground. He is warm too; and from the short knowledge I have of him, I will pledge myself for his veracity: if what he reports of himself were not true, he would not utter it—and for me, youth, I honour a frankness which becomes thy birth. But now, and thou didst offend me; yet the noble blood which flows in thy veins may well be allowed to boil out, when it has so recently traced itself to its source. Come, my lord, [turning to Manfred] if I can pardon him, surely you may: it is not the youth's fault, if you took him for a spectre. This bitter taunt galled the soul of Manfred. If beings from an-other world, replied he haughtily, have power to impress my mind with awe, it is more than living man can do; nor could a stripling's arm——My lord, interrupted Hippolita, your guest has occasion for repose; shall we not leave him to his rest? Saying this, and taking Manfred by the hand, she took leave of Frederic, and led the company forth. The prince, not sorry to quit a conversation which recalled to mind the discovery he had made of his most secret sensa-tions, suffered himself to be conducted to his own apart-ment, after permitting Theodore, though under engagement to return to the castle on the morrow, [a condition the young man gladly accepted] to retire with his father to the

convent. Matilda and Isabella were too much occupied with
their own reflections, and too little content with each other,
to wish for farther converse that night. They separated each
to her chamber, with more expressions of ceremony, and
fewer of affection, than had passed between them since their
childhood.

If they parted with small cordiality, they did but meet
with greater impatience as soon as the sun was risen. Their
minds were in a situation that excluded sleep, and each
recollected a thousand questions which she wished she had
put to the other overnight. Matilda reflected that Isabella
had been twice delivered by Theodore in very critical situations, which she could not believe accidental. His eyes, it
was true, had been fixed on her in Frederic's chamber; but
that might have been to disguise his passion for Isabella
from the fathers of both. It were better to clear this up. She
wished to know the truth, lest she should wrong her friend
by entertaining a passion for Isabella's lover. Thus jealousy
prompted, and at the same time borrowed an excuse from
friendship to justify its curiosity.

Isabella, not less restless, had better foundation for her
suspicions. Both Theodore's tongue and eyes had told her
his heart was engaged, it was true—yet perhaps Matilda
might not correspond to his passion—She had ever appeared insensible to love; all her thoughts were set on
heaven—Why did I dissuade her? said Isabella to herself; I
am punished for my generosity—But when did they meet?
where?—It cannot be; I have deceived myself.—Perhaps
last night was the first time they ever beheld each other—it
must be some other object that has prepossessed his affections—If it is, I am not so unhappy as I thought; if it is not
my friend Matilda—How! can I stoop to wish for the affection of a man, who rudely and unnecessarily acquainted me
with his indifference? and that at the very moment in which
common courtesy demanded at least expressions of civility.
I will go to my dear Matilda, who will confirm me in this

becoming pride—Man is false—I will advise with her on
taking the veil: she will rejoice to find me in this disposition;
and I will acquaint her that I no longer oppose her inclination for the cloister. In this frame of mind, and determined
to open her heart entirely to Matilda, she went to that
princess's chamber, whom she found already dressed, and
leaning pensively on her arm. This attitude, so correspond-
ent to what she felt herself, revived Isabella's suspicions, and
destroyed the confidence she had purposed to place in her
friend. They blushed at meeting, and were too much novices
to disguise their sensations with address. After some
unmeaning questions and replies, Matilda demanded of
Isabella the cause of her flight. The latter, who had almost
forgotten Manfred's passion, so entirely was she occupied
by her own, concluding that Matilda referred to her last
escape from the convent, which had occasioned the events
of the preceding evening, replied, Martelli brought word to
the convent that your mother was dead.—Oh! said Matilda
interrupting her, Bianca has explained that mistake to me:
on seeing me faint, she cried out, The princess is dead! and
Martelli, who had come for the usual dole to the castle——
And what made you faint? said Isabella, indifferent to the
rest. Matilda blushed, and stammered—My father—he was
sitting in judgment on a criminal.—What criminal? said
Isabella eagerly.——A young man, said Matilda—I believe—I think it was that young man that—What,
Theodore? said Isabella. Yes, answered she; I never saw him
before; I do not know how he had offended my father—but,
as he has been of service to you, I am glad my lord has
pardoned him. Served me? replied Isabella: do you term it
serving me, to wound my father, and almost occasion his
death? Though it is but since yesterday that I am blessed
with knowing a parent, I hope Matilda does not think I am
such a stranger to filial tenderness as not to resent the boldness of that audacious youth, and that it is impossible for me
ever to feel any affection for one who dared to lift his arm

against the author of my being. No, Matilda, my heart abhors him; and if you still retain the friendship for me that you have vowed from your infancy, you will detest a man who has been on the point of making me miserable for ever. Matilda held down her head, and replied, I hope my dearest Isabella does not doubt her Matilda's friendship: I never beheld that youth until yesterday; he is almost a stranger to me: but as the surgeons have pronounced your father out of danger, you ought not to harbour uncharitable resentment against one who I am persuaded did not know the marquis was related to you. You plead his cause very pathetically, said Isabella, considering he is so much a stranger to you! I am mistaken, or he returns your charity. What mean you? said Matilda. Nothing, said Isabella; repenting that she had given Matilda a hint of Theodore's inclination for her. Then changing the discourse, she asked Matilda what occasioned Manfred to take Theodore for a spectre? Bless me, said Matilda, did not you observe his extreme resemblance to the portrait of Alfonso in the gallery? I took notice of it to Bianca even before I saw him in armour; but with the helmet on, he is the very image of that picture. I do not much observe pictures, said Isabella; much less have I examined this young man so attentively as you seem to have done. ——Ah! Matilda, your heart is in danger—but let me warn you as a friend—He has owned to me that he is in love: it cannot be with you, for yesterday was the first time you ever met—was it not? Certainly, replied Matilda. But why does my dearest Isabella conclude from any thing I have said, that—She paused—then continuing, He saw you first, and I am far from having the vanity to think that my little portion of charms could engage a heart devoted to you. May you be happy, Isabella, whatever is the fate of Matilda!— My lovely friend, said Isabella, whose heart was too honest to resist a kind expression, it is you that Theodore admires; I saw it; I am persuaded of it; nor shall a thought of my own happiness suffer me to interfere with yours. This frankness drew tears from the gentle Matilda; and jealousy, that for a moment had raised a coolness between these amiable maidens, soon gave way to the natural sincerity and candour of their souls. Each confessed to the other the impression that Theodore had made on her; and this confidence was followed by a struggle of generosity, each insisting on yielding her claim to her friend. At length, the dignity of Isabella's virtue reminding her of the preference which Theodore had almost declared for her rival, made her determine to conquer her passion, and cede the beloved object to her friend.

During this contest of amity, Hippolita entered her daughter's chamber. Madam, said she to Isabella, you have so much tenderness for Matilda, and interest yourself so kindly in whatever affects our wretched house, that I can have no secrets with my child, which are not proper for you to hear. The princesses were all attention and anxiety. Know then, madam, continued Hippolita, and you, my dearest Matilda, that being convinced by all the events of these two last ominous days, that heaven purposes the sceptre of Otranto should pass from Manfred's hands into those of the marquis Frederic, I have been perhaps inspired with the thought of averting our total destruction by the union of our rival houses. With this view I have been proposing to Manfred my lord to tender this dear dear child to Frederic your father—Me to lord Frederic! cried Matilda—Good heavens! my gracious mother—and have you named it to my father? I have, said Hippolita: he listened benignly to my proposal, and is gone to break it to the marquis. Ah! wretched princess! cried Isabella, what hast thou done? What ruin has thy inadvertent goodness been preparing for thyself, for me, and for Matilda! Ruin from me to you and to my child! said Hippolita: What can this mean? Alas! said Isabella, the purity of your own heart prevents your seeing the depravity of others. Manfred, your lord, that impious man——Hold, said Hippolita; you must not in my presence, young lady, mention Manfred with disrespect: he is my lord and husband, and—Will not be long so, said Isabella, if his wicked purposes can be carried into execution. This language amazes me, said Hippolita. Your feeling, Isabella, is warm; but until this hour I never knew it betray you into intemperance. What deed of Manfred authorizes you to treat him as a murderer, an assassin? Thou virtuous and too credulous princess! replied Isabella; it is not thy life he aims at—it is to separate himself from thee! to divorce thee! To—to divorce me! To divorce my mother! cried Hippolita and Matilda at once.—Yes, said Isabella; and to complete his crime, he meditates—I cannot speak it! What can surpass what thou hast already uttered? said Matilda. Hippolita was silent. Grief choked her speech: and the recollection of Manfred's late ambiguous discourses confirmed what she heard. Excellent, dear lady! madam! mother! cried Isabella, flinging herself at Hippolita's feet in a transport of passion; trust me, believe me, I will die a thousand deaths sooner than consent to injure you, than yield to so odious— oh!—This is too much! cried Hippolita: what crimes does one crime suggest! Rise, dear Isabella; I do not doubt your virtue. Oh! Matilda, this stroke is too heavy for thee! Weep not, my child; and not a murmur, I charge thee. Remember, he is *thy* father still.—But you are my mother too, said Matilda fervently; and *you* are virtuous, *you* are guiltless!— Oh! must not I, must not I complain? You must not, said Hippolita—Come, all will yet be well. Manfred, in the agony for the loss of thy brother, knew not what he said: perhaps Isabella misunderstood him: his heart is good— and, my child, thou knowest not all. There is a destiny hangs over us; the hand of Providence is stretched out— Oh! could I but save thee from the wreck!—Yes, continued she in a firmer tone, perhaps the sacrifice of myself may atone for all——I will go and offer myself to this divorce— it boots not what becomes of me. I will withdraw into the neighbouring monastery, and waste the remainder of life in

prayers and tears for my child and—the prince! Thou art as much too good for this world, said Isabella, as Manfred is execrable—But think not, lady, that thy weakness shall determine for me. I swear—hear me, all ye angels——Stop, I adjure thee, cried Hippolita; remember, thou dost not depend on thyself; thou hast a father.—My father is too pious, too noble, interrupted Isabella, to command an impious deed. But should he command it, can a father enjoin a cursed act? I was contracted to the son; can I wed the father?—No, madam, no; force should not drag me to Manfred's hated bed. I loathe him, I abhor him: divine and human laws forbid.—And my friend, my dearest Matilda! would I wound her tender soul by injuring her adored mother? my own mother—I never have known another.—
—Oh! she is the mother of both! cried Matilda. Can we, can we, Isabella, adore her too much? My lovely children, said the touched Hippolita, your tenderness overpowers me—but I must not give way to it. It is not ours to make election for ourselves; heaven, our fathers, and our husbands, must decide for us. Have patience until you hear what Manfred and Frederic have determined. If the marquis accepts Matilda's hand, I know she will readily obey. Heaven may interpose and prevent the rest. What means my child? continued she, seeing Matilda fall at her feet with a flood of speechless tears—But no; answer me not, my daughter; I must not hear a word against the pleasure of thy father. Oh! doubt not my obedience, my dreadful obedience to him and to you! said Matilda. But can I, most respected of women, can I experience all this tenderness, this world of goodness, and conceal a thought from the best of mothers? What art thou going to utter? said Isabella trembling. Recollect thyself, Matilda. No, Isabella, said the princess, I should not deserve this incomparable parent, if the inmost recesses of my soul harboured a thought without her permission— Nay, I have offended her; I have suffered a passion to enter my heart without her avowal—But here I disclaim it; here

I vow to heaven and her——My child! my child! said
Hippolita, what words are these? What new calamities has
fate in store for us? Thou, a passion! thou, in this hour of
destruction——Oh! I see all my guilt! said Matilda. I abhor
myself, if I cost my mother a pang. She is the dearest thing
I have on earth—Oh! I will never, never behold him more!
Isabella, said Hippolita, thou art conscious to this unhappy
secret, whatever it is. Speak—What! cried Matilda, have I so
forfeited my mother's love that she will not permit me even
to speak my own guilt? Oh! wretched, wretched Matilda!—
Thou art too cruel, said Isabella to Hippolita: canst thou
behold this anguish of a virtuous mind, and not commiser-
ate it? Not pity my child! said Hippolita, catching Matilda
in her arms—Oh! I know she is good, she is all virtue, all
tenderness, and duty. I do forgive thee, my excellent, my
only hope! The princesses then revealed to Hippolita their
mutual inclination for Theodore, and the purpose of
Isabella to resign him to Matilda. Hippolita blamed their
imprudence, and shewed them the improbability that either
father would consent to bestow his heiress on so poor a
man, though nobly born. Some comfort it gave her to find
their passion of so recent a date, and that Theodore had but
little cause to suspect it in either. She strictly enjoined them
to avoid all correspondence with him. This Matilda fervently promised: but Isabella, who flattered herself that she
meant no more than to promote his union with her friend,
could not determine to avoid him; and made no reply. I will
go to the convent, said Hippolita, and order new masses to
be said for a deliverance from these calamities.—Oh! my
mother, said Matilda, you mean to quit us: you mean to take
sanctuary, and to give my father an opportunity of pursuing
his fatal intention. Alas! on my knees I supplicate you to
forbear—Will you leave me a prey to Frederic? I will follow
you to the convent.—Be at peace, my child, said Hippolita:
I will return instantly. I will never abandon thee, until I
know it is the will of heaven, and for thy benefit. Do not

deceive me, said Matilda. I will not marry Frederic until thou commandest it. Alas! what will become of me!—Why that exclamation! said Hippolita. I have promised thee to return.—Ah! my mother, replied Matilda, stay and save me from myself. A frown from thee can do more than all my father's severity. I have given away my heart, and you alone can make me recall it. No more, said Hippolita: thou must not relapse, Matilda. I can quit Theodore, said she, but must I wed another? Let me attend thee to the altar, and shut myself from the world forever. Thy fate depends on thy father, said Hippolita: I have ill bestowed my tenderness, if it has taught thee to revere aught beyond him. Adieu, my child! I go to pray for thee.

Hippolita's real purpose was to demand of Jerome, whether in conscience she might not consent to the divorce. She had oft urged Manfred to resign the principality, which the delicacy of her conscience rendered an hourly burthen to her. These scruples concurred to make the separation from her husband appear less dreadful to her than it would have seemed in any other situation.

Jerome, at quitting the castle overnight, had questioned Theodore severely why he had accused him to Manfred of being privy to his escape. Theodore owned it had been with design to prevent Manfred's suspicion from alighting on Matilda; and added, the holiness of Jerome's life and character secured him from the tyrant's wrath. Jerome was heartily grieved to discover his son's inclination for that princess; and, leaving him to his rest, promised in the morning to acquaint him with important reasons for conquering his passion. Theodore, like Isabella, was too recently acquainted with parental authority to submit to its decisions against the impulse of his heart. He had little curiosity to learn the friar's reasons, and less disposition to obey them. The lovely Matilda had made stronger impressions on him than filial affection. All night he pleased himself with visions of love; and it was not till late after the morning-office, that he recollected the friar's commands to attend him at Alfonso's tomb.

Young man, said Jerome, when he saw him, this tardiness does not please me. Have a father's commands already so little weight? Theodore made awkward excuses, and attributed his delay to having overslept himself. And on whom were thy dreams employed? said the friar sternly. His son blushed. Come, come, resumed the friar, inconsiderate youth, this must not be; eradicate this guilty passion from thy breast.—Guilty passion! cried Theodore: can guilt dwell with innocent beauty and virtuous modesty? It is sinful, replied the friar, to cherish those whom heaven has doomed to destruction. A tyrant's race must be swept from the earth to the third and fourth generation. Will heaven visit the innocent for the crimes of the guilty?* said Theodore. The fair Matilda has virtues enough—To undo thee, interrupted Jerome. Hast thou so soon forgotten that twice the savage Manfred has pronounced thy sentence? Nor have I forgotten, sir, said Theodore, that the charity of his daughter delivered me from his power. I can forget injuries, but never benefits. The injuries thou hast received from Manfred's race, said the friar, are beyond what thou canst conceive.—Reply not, but view this holy image! Beneath this marble monument rest the ashes of the good Alfonso; a prince adorned with every virtue: the father of his people! the delight of mankind! Kneel, headstrong boy, and list, while a father unfolds a tale of horror, that will expel every sentiment from thy soul, but sensations of sacred vengeance.—Alfonso! much-injured prince! let thy unsatisfied shade sit awful on the troubled air, while these trembling lips—Ha! who comes there?—The most wretched of women, said Hippolita, entering the choir. Good father, art thou at leisure?—But why this kneeling youth? what means the horror imprinted on each countenance? why at this venerable tomb—Alas! hast thou seen aught? We were pouring forth our orisons to heaven, replied the friar with some confusion, to put an end to the woes of this deplorable province. Join with us, lady! thy spotless soul may obtain an exemption from the judgments which the portents of these days but too speakingly denounce against thy house. I pray fervently to heaven to divert them, said the pious princess. Thou knowest it has been the occupation of my life to wrest a blessing for my lord and my harmless children—One, alas! is taken from me! Would heaven but hear me for my poor Matilda! Father, intercede for her!—Every heart will bless her, cried Theodore with rapture.—Be dumb, rash youth! said Jerome. And thou, fond princess, contend not with the powers above! The Lord giveth, and the Lord taketh away: bless his holy name, and submit to his decrees. I do most devoutly, said Hippolita: but will he not spare my only comfort? must Matilda perish too?—Ah! father, I came—But dismiss thy son. No ear but thine must hear what I have to utter. May heaven grant thy every wish, most excellent princess! said Theodore retiring. Jerome frowned.

Hippolita then acquainted the friar with the proposal she had suggested to Manfred, his approbation of it, and the tender of Matilda that he was gone to make to Frederic. Jerome could not conceal his dislike of the motion, which he covered under pretence of the improbability that Frederic, the nearest of blood to Alfonso, and who was come to claim his succession, would yield to an alliance with the usurper of his right. But nothing could equal the perplexity of the friar, when Hippolita confessed her readiness not to oppose the separation, and demanded his opinion on the legality of her acquiescence. The friar catched eagerly at her request of his advice; and without explaining his aversion to the proposed marriage of Manfred and Isabella, he painted to Hippolita in the most alarming colours the sinfulness of her consent, denounced judgments against her if she complied, and enjoined her in the severest terms to treat any such proposition with every mark of indignation and refusal.

Manfred, in the mean time, had broken his purpose to Frederic, and proposed the double marriage. That weak prince, who had been struck with the charms of Matilda, listened but too eagerly to the offer. He forgot his enmity to Manfred, whom he saw but little hope of dispossessing by force; and flattering himself that no issue might succeed from the union of his daughter with the tyrant, he looked upon his own succession to the principality as facilitated by wedding Matilda. He made faint opposition to the proposal; affecting, for form only, not to acquiesce unless Hippolita should consent to the divorce. Manfred took that upon himself. Transported with his success, and impatient to see himself in a situation to expect sons, he hastened to his wife's apartment, determined to extort her compliance. He learned with indignation that she was absent at the convent. His guilt suggested to him that she had probably been informed by Isabella of his purpose. He doubted whether her retirement to the convent did not import an intention of remaining there, until she could raise obstacles to their divorce; and the suspicions he had already entertained of Jerome, made him apprehend that the friar would not only traverse his views, but might have inspired Hippolita with the resolution of taking sanctuary. Impatient to unravel this clue, and to defeat its success, Manfred hastened to the convent, and arrived there as the friar was earnestly exhorting the princess never to yield to the divorce.

Madam, said Manfred, what business drew you hither? Why did not you await my return from the marquis? I came to implore a blessing on your councils, replied Hippolita. My councils do not need a friar's intervention, said Manfred—and of all men living is that hoary traitor the only one whom you delight to confer with? Profane prince! said Jerome: is it at the altar that thou choosest to insult the servants of the altar?—But, Manfred, thy impious schemes are known. Heaven and this virtuous lady know them. Nay, frown not, prince. The church despises thy menaces. Her thunders will be heard above thy wrath. Dare to proceed in thy curst purpose of a divorce, until her sentence be known, and here I lance her anathema* at thy head. Audacious rebel! said Manfred, endeavouring to conceal the awe with which the friar's words inspired him; dost thou presume to threaten thy lawful prince? Thou art no lawful prince, said Jerome; thou art no prince—Go, discuss thy claim with Frederic, and when that is done—It is done, replied Manfred: Frederic accepts Matilda's hand, and is content to wave his claim, unless I have no male issue.—As he spoke those words three drops of blood fell from the nose of Alfonso's statue.* Manfred turned pale, and the princess sunk on her knees. Behold! said the friar: mark this miraculous indication that the blood of Alfonso will never mix with that of Manfred! My gracious lord, said Hippolita, let us submit ourselves to heaven. Think not thy ever obedient wife rebels against thy authority. I have no will but that of my lord and the church. To that revered tribunal let us appeal. It does not depend on us to burst the bonds that unite us. If the church shall approve the dissolution of our marriage, be it so—I have but few years, and those of sorrow, to pass. Where can they be worn away so well as at the foot of this altar, in prayers for thine and Matilda's safety?—But thou shalt not remain here until then, said Manfred. Repair with me to the castle, and there I will advise on the proper measures for a divorce.—But this meddling friar comes not thither; my hospitable roof shall never more harbour a traitor—and for thy reverence's offspring, continued he, I banish him from my dominions. He, I ween, is no sacred personage, nor under the protection of the church. Whoever weds Isabella, it shall not be father Falconara's started-up son. They start up, said the friar, who are suddenly beheld in the seat of lawful princes; but they wither away like the grass, and their place knows them

no more.* Manfred, casting a look of scorn at the friar, led
Hippolita forth; but at the door of the church whispered
one of his attendants to remain concealed about the convent, and bring him instant notice, if any one from the castle
should repair thither.

# CHAPTER V

EVERY reflection which Manfred made on the friar's behaviour, conspired to persuade him that Jerome was privy
to an amour between Isabella and Theodore. But Jerome's
new presumption, so dissonant from his former meekness,
suggested still deeper apprehensions. The prince even suspected that the friar depended on some secret support from
Frederic, whose arrival coinciding with the novel appearance of Theodore seemed to bespeak a correspondence. Still
more was he troubled with the resemblance of Theodore to
Alfonso's portrait. The latter he knew had unquestionably
died without issue. Frederic had consented to bestow
Isabella on him. These contradictions agitated his mind with
numberless pangs. He saw but two methods of extricating
himself from his difficulties. The one was to resign his dominions to the marquis.—Pride, ambition, and his reliance
on ancient prophecies,* which had pointed out a possibility
of his preserving them to his posterity, combated that
thought. The other was to press his marriage with Isabella.
After long ruminating on these anxious thoughts, as he
marched silently with Hippolita to the castle, he at last
discoursed with that princess on the subject of his disquiet,
and used every insinuating and plausible argument to
extract her consent to, even her promise of promoting,
the divorce. Hippolita needed little persuasion to bend her
to his pleasure. She endeavoured to win him over to the
measure of resigning his dominions; but finding her exhortations fruitless, she assured him, that as far as her conscience would allow, she would raise no opposition to a
separation, though, without better founded scruples than
what he yet alleged, she would not engage to be active in
demanding it.

This compliance, though inadequate, was sufficient to

raise Manfred's hopes. He trusted that his power and wealth would easily advance his suit at the court of Rome, whither he resolved to engage Frederic to take a journey on purpose. That prince had discovered so much passion for Matilda, that Manfred hoped to obtain all he wished by holding out or withdrawing his daughter's charms, according as the marquis should appear more or less disposed to co-operate in his views. Even the absence of Frederic would be a material point gained, until he could take farther measures for his security.

Dismissing Hippolita to her apartment, he repaired to that of the marquis; but crossing the great hall through which he was to pass, he met Bianca. That damsel he knew was in the confidence of both the young ladies. It immediately occurred to him to sift her on the subject of Isabella and Theodore. Calling her aside into the recess of the oriel window* of the hall, and soothing her with many fair words and promises, he demanded of her whether she knew aught of the state of Isabella's affections. I! my lord? No, my lord—Yes, my lord—Poor lady! she is wonderfully alarmed about her father's wounds; but I tell her he will do well; don't your highness think so? I do not ask you, replied Manfred, what she thinks about her father: but you are in her secrets: come, be a good girl and tell me, is there any young man—ha?—you understand me. Lord bless me! understand your highness? No, not I: I told her a few vulnerary herbs* and repose——I am not talking, replied the prince impatiently, about her father: I know he will do well. Bless me, I rejoice to hear your highness say so; for though I thought it right not to let my young lady despond, methought his greatness had a wan look, and a something— I remember when young Ferdinand was wounded by the Venetian. Thou answerest from the point, interrupted Manfred; but here, take this jewel, perhaps that may fix thy attention—Nay, no reverences; my favour shall not stop here—Come, tell me truly; how stands Isabella's heart?

Well, your highness has such a way, said Bianca—to be
sure—but can your highness keep a secret? If it should ever
come out of your lips——It shall not, it shall not, cried
Manfred. Nay, but swear, your highness—by my
halidame,* if it should ever be known that I said it—Why,
truth is truth, I do not think my lady Isabella ever much
affectioned my young lord, your son: yet he was a sweet
youth as one should see. I am sure if I had been a princess—
But bless me! I must attend my lady Matilda; she will marvel what is become of me.—Stay, cried Manfred, thou hast
not satisfied my question. Hast thou ever carried any message, any letter?—I! Good gracious! cried Bianca: I carry a
letter? I would not to be a queen. I hope your highness
thinks, though I am poor, I am honest.* Did your highness
never hear what count Marsigli offered me, when he came
a-wooing to my lady Matilda?—I have not leisure, said
Manfred, to listen to thy tales. I do not question thy honesty; but it is thy duty to conceal nothing from me. How
long has Isabella been acquainted with Theodore?—Nay,
there is nothing can escape your highness, said Bianca—not
that I know any thing of the matter. Theodore, to be sure, is
a proper young man, and, as my lady Matilda says, the very
image of good Alfonso: Has not your highness remarked it?
Yes, yes—No—thou torturest me, said Manfred: Where did
they meet? when?—Who, my lady Matilda? said Bianca.
No, no, not Matilda; Isabella: When did Isabella first become acquainted with this Theodore?—Virgin Mary! said
Bianca, how should I know? Thou dost know, said
Manfred; and I must know; I will.—Lord! your highness is
not jealous of young Theodore? said Bianca.—Jealous! No,
no: why should I be jealous?—Perhaps I mean to unite
them—if I was sure Isabella would have no repugnance.—
Repugnance! No, I'll warrant her, said Bianca: he is as
comely a youth as ever trod on christian ground: we are all
in love with him: there is not a soul in the castle but would
be rejoiced to have him for our prince—I mean, when it

shall please heaven to call your highness to itself.—Indeed! said Manfred: has it gone so far? Oh! this cursed friar!—But I must not lose time—Go, Bianca, attend Isabella; but I charge thee, not a word of what has passed. Find out how she is affected towards Theodore; bring me good news, and that ring has a companion. Wait at the foot of the winding staircase: I am going to visit the marquis, and will talk farther with thee at my return.

Manfred, after some general conversation, desired Frederic to dismiss the two knights his companions, having to talk with him on urgent affairs. As soon as they were alone, he began in artful guise to sound the marquis on the subject of Matilda; and finding him disposed to his wish, he let drop hints on the difficulties that would attend the celebration of their marriage, unless——At that instant Bianca burst into the room, with a wildness in her look and gestures that spoke the utmost terror. Oh! my lord, my lord! cried she, we are all undone! It is come again! it is come again!—What is come again? cried Manfred amazed.—Oh! the hand! the giant! the hand!—Support me! I am terrified out of my senses, cried Bianca: I will not sleep in the castle to-night. Where shall I go? My things may come after me to-morrow.—Would I had been content to wed Francesco! This comes of ambition!—What has terrified thee thus, young woman? said the marquis: thou art safe here; be not alarmed. Oh! your greatness is wonderfully good, said Bianca, but I dare not—No, pray let me go—I had rather leave every thing behind me, than stay another hour under this roof. Go to, thou hast lost thy senses, said Manfred. Interrupt us not; we were communing on important matters.—My lord, this wench is subject to fits—Come with me, Bianca.—Oh! the saints! No, said Bianca—for certain it comes to warn your highness; why should it appear to me else! I say my prayers morning and evening—Oh! if your highness had believed Diego! 'Tis the same hand that he saw the foot to in the gallery-chamber—Father Jerome has often

told us the prophecy would be out one of these days—
Bianca, said he, mark my words.—Thou ravest, said
Manfred in a rage: Begone, and keep these fooleries to
frighten thy companions.—What! my lord, cried Bianca, do
you think I have seen nothing? Go to the foot of the great
stairs yourself—As I live I saw it. Saw what? Tell us fair
maid, what thou hast seen, said Frederic. Can your highness
listen, said Manfred, to the delirium of a silly wench, who
has heard stories of apparitions until she believes them?
This is more than fancy, said the marquis; her terror is too
natural and too strongly impressed to be the work of imagination. Tell us, fair maiden, what it is has moved thee thus.
Yes, my lord, thank your greatness, said Bianca—I believe
I look very pale; I shall be better when I have recovered
myself.—I was going to my lady Isabella's chamber by his
highness's order—We do not want the circumstances, interrupted Manfred: since his highness will have it so, proceed;
but be brief.—Lord, your highness thwarts one so! replied
Bianca—I fear my hair—I am sure I never in my life—Well!
as I was telling your greatness, I was going by his highness's
order to my lady Isabella's chamber: she lies in the watchet-
coloured chamber,* on the right hand, one pair of stairs: so
when I came to the great stairs—I was looking on his highness's present here. Grant me patience! said Manfred, will
this wench never come to the point? What imports it to the
marquis, that I gave thee a bawble for thy faithful attend-
ance on my daughter? We want to know what thou sawest.
I was going to tell your highness, said Bianca, if you would
permit me.—So, as I was rubbing the ring—I am sure I had
not gone up three steps, but I heard the rattling of armour;
for all the world such a clatter, as Diego says he heard when
the giant turned him about in the gallery-chamber.—What
does she mean, my lord!? said the marquis. Is your castle
haunted by giants and goblins?—Lord, what, has not your
greatness heard the story of the giant in the gallery-
chamber? cried Bianca. I marvel his highness has not told

you—mayhap you do not know there is a prophecy—This trifling is intolerable, interrupted Manfred. Let us dismiss this silly wench, my lord: we have more important affairs to discuss. By your favour, said Frederic, these are no trifles: the enormous sabre I was directed to in the wood; yon casque, its fellow—are these visions of this poor maiden's brain?—So Jaquez thinks, may it please your greatness, said Bianca. He says this moon will not be out without our seeing some strange revolution. For my part, I should not be surprised if it was to happen to-morrow; for, as I was saying, when I heard the clattering of armour, I was all in a cold sweat—I looked up, and, if your greatness will believe me, I saw upon the uppermost banister of the great stairs a hand in armour as big, as big—I thought I should have swooned—I never stopped until I came hither—Would I were well out of this castle! My lady Matilda told me but yester-morning that her highness Hippolita knows something—Thou art an insolent! cried Manfred—Lord marquis, it much misgives me that this scene is concerted to affront me. Are my own domestics suborned to spread tales injurious to my honour? Pursue your claim by manly daring; or let us bury our feuds, as was proposed, by the intermarriage of our children: but trust me, it ill becomes a prince of your bearing to practise on mercenary wenches.— I scorn your imputation, said Frederic; until this hour I never set eyes on this damsel: I have given her no jewel!— My lord, my lord, your conscience, your guilt accuses you, and would throw the suspicion on me—But keep your daughter, and think no more of Isabella: the judgments already fallen on your house forbid me matching into it.

Manfred, alarmed at the resolute tone in which Frederic delivered these words, endeavoured to pacify him. Dismissing Bianca, he made such submissions to the marquis, and threw in such artful encomiums on Matilda, that Frederic was once more staggered. However, as his passion was of so recent a date, it could not at once surmount the scruples he had conceived. He had gathered enough from Bianca's discourse to persuade him that heaven declared itself against Manfred. The proposed marriages too removed his claim to a distance: and the principality of Otranto was a stronger temptation, than the contingent reversion of it with Matilda. Still he would not absolutely recede from his engagements; but purposing to gain time, he demanded of Manfred if it was true in fact that Hippolita consented to the divorce. The prince, transported to find no other obstacle, and depending on his influence over his wife, assured the marquis it was so, and that he might satisfy himself of the truth from her own mouth.

As they were thus discoursing, word was brought that the banquet was prepared. Manfred conducted Frederic to the great hall, where they were received by Hippolita and the young princesses. Manfred placed the marquis next to Matilda, and seated himself between his wife and Isabella. Hippolita comported herself with an easy gravity; but the young ladies were silent and melancholy. Manfred, who was determined to pursue his point with the marquis in the remainder of the evening, pushed on the feast until it waxed late; affecting unrestrained gaiety, and plying Frederic with repeated goblets of wine. The latter, more upon his guard than Manfred wished, declined his frequent challenges, on pretence of his late loss of blood; while the prince, to raise his own disordered spirits, and to counterfeit unconcern, indulged himself in plentiful draughts, though not to the intoxication of his senses.

The evening being far advanced, the banquet concluded. Manfred would have withdrawn with Frederic; but the latter, pleading weakness and want of repose, retired to his chamber, gallantly telling the prince, that his daughter should amuse his highness until himself could attend him. Manfred accepted the party; and, to the no small grief of

Isabella, accompanied her to her apartment. Matilda waited on her mother, to enjoy the freshness of the evening on the ramparts of the castle.

Soon as the company was dispersed their several ways, Frederic, quitting his chamber, enquired if Hippolita was alone; and was told by one of her attendants, who had not noticed her going forth, that at that hour she generally withdrew to her oratory, where he probably would find her. The marquis during the repast had beheld Matilda with increase of passion. He now wished to find Hippolita in the disposition her lord had promised. The portents that had alarmed him were forgotten in his desires. Stealing softly and unobserved to the apartment of Hippolita, he entered it with a resolution to encourage her acquiescence to the divorce, having perceived that Manfred was resolved to make the possession of Isabella an unalterable condition, before he would grant Matilda to his wishes.

The marquis was not surprised at the silence that reigned in the princess's apartment. Concluding her, as he had been advertised,* in her oratory, he passed on. The door was a-jar; the evening gloomy and overcast. Pushing open the door gently, he saw a person kneeling before the altar. As he approached nearer, it seemed not a woman, but one in a long woollen weed, whose back was towards him. The person seemed absorbed in prayer. The marquis was about to return, when the figure rising, stood some moments fixed in meditation, without regarding him. The marquis, expecting the holy person to come forth, and meaning to excuse his uncivil interruption, said, Reverend father, I sought the lady Hippolita.—Hippolita! replied a hollow voice: camest thou to this castle to seek Hippolita?—And then the figure, turning slowly round, discovered to Frederic the fleshless jaws and empty sockets of a skeleton, wrapt in a hermit's cowl. Angels of grace, protect me!* cried Frederic recoiling. Deserve their protection, said the spectre. Frederic, falling on his knees, adjured the phantom to take pity on him. Dost thou not remember me? said the apparition. Remember the wood of Joppa! Art thou that holy hermit? cried Frederic trembling—can I do aught for thy eternal peace?—Wast thou delivered from bondage, said the spectre, to pursue carnal delights? Hast thou forgotten the buried sabre, and the behest of heaven engraven on it?—I have not, I have not, said Frederic—But say, blest spirit, what is thy errand to me? what remains to be done? To forget Matilda! said the apparition—and vanished.

Frederic's blood froze in his veins. For some minutes he remained motionless. Then falling prostrate on his face before the altar, he besought the intercession of every saint for pardon. A flood of tears succeeded to this transport; and the image of the beauteous Matilda rushing in spite of him on his thoughts, he lay on the ground in a conflict of penitence and passion. Ere he could recover from this agony of his spirits, the princess Hippolita, with a taper in her hand, entered the oratory alone. Seeing a man without motion on the floor, she gave a shriek, concluding him dead. Her fright brought Frederic to himself. Rising suddenly, his face bedewed with tears, he would have rushed from her presence; but Hippolita, stopping him, conjured him in the most plaintive accents to explain the cause of his disorder, and by what strange chance she had found him there in that posture. Ah! virtuous princess! said the marquis, penetrated with grief—and stopped. For the love of heaven, my lord, said Hippolita, disclose the cause of this transport! What mean these doleful sounds, this alarming exclamation on my name? What woes has heaven still in store for the wretched Hippolita?—Yet silent?—By every pitying angel, I adjure thee, noble prince, continued she, falling at his feet, to disclose the purport of what lies at thy heart—I see thou feelest for me; thou feelest the sharp pangs that thou inflictest—Speak, for pity!—Does aught thou knowest concern my child?—I cannot speak, cried Frederic, bursting from her—Oh! Matilda!

Quitting the princess thus abruptly, he hastened to his own apartment. At the door of it he was accosted by Manfred, who, flushed by wine and love, had come to seek him, and to propose to waste some hours of the night in music and revelling. Frederic, offended at an invitation so dissonant from the mood of his soul, pushed him rudely aside, and, entering his chamber, flung the door intemperately against Manfred, and bolted it inwards. The haughty prince, enraged at this unaccountable behaviour, withdrew in a frame of mind capable of the most fatal excesses. As he crossed the court, he was met by the domestic whom he had planted at the convent as a spy on Jerome and Theodore. This man, almost breathless with the haste he had made, informed his lord, that Theodore and some lady from the castle were at that instant in private conference at the tomb of Alfonso in St. Nicholas's church. He had dogged Theodore thither, but the gloominess of the night had prevented his discovering who the woman was.

Manfred, whose spirits were inflamed, and whom Isabella had driven from her on his urging his passion with too little reserve, did not doubt but the inquietude she had expressed had been occasioned by her impatience to meet Theodore. Provoked by this conjecture, and enraged at her father, he hastened secretly to the great church. Gliding softly between the aisles, and guided by an imperfect gleam of moonshine that shone faintly through the illuminated windows, he stole towards the tomb of Alfonso, to which he was directed by indistinct whispers of the persons he sought. The first sounds he could distinguish were—Does it, alas, depend on me? Manfred will never permit our union.—No, this shall prevent it! cried the tyrant, drawing his dagger, and plunging it over her shoulder into the bosom of the person that spoke—Ah me, I am slain! cried Matilda sinking: Good heaven, receive my soul!—Savage, inhuman monster! what hast thou done? cried Theodore, rushing on him, and wrenching his dagger from him.—Stop, stop thy impious hand, cried Matilda; it is my father!—Manfred, waking as from a trance, beat his breast, twisted his hands in his locks, and endeavoured to recover his dagger from Theodore to dispatch himself. Theodore, scarce less distracted, and only mastering the transports of his grief to assist Matilda, had now by his cries drawn some of the monks to his aid. While part of them endeavoured in concert with the afflicted Theodore to stop the blood of the dying princess, the rest prevented Manfred from laying violent hands on himself.

Matilda, resigning herself patiently to her fate, acknowledged with looks of grateful love the zeal of Theodore. Yet oft as her faintness would permit her speech its way, she begged the assistants to comfort her father. Jerome by this time had learnt the fatal news, and reached the church. His looks seemed to reproach Theodore; but turning to Manfred, he said, Now, tyrant! behold the completion of woe fulfilled on thy impious and devoted head! The blood of Alfonso cried to heaven for vengeance; and heaven has permitted its altar to be polluted by assassination, that thou mightest shed thy own blood at the foot of that prince's sepulchre!—Cruel man! cried Matilda, to aggravate the woes of a parent! May heaven bless my father, and forgive him as I do! My lord, my gracious sire, dost thou forgive thy child? Indeed I came not hither to meet Theodore! I found him praying at this tomb, whither my mother sent me to intercede for thee, for her—Dearest father, bless your child, and say you forgive her.—Forgive thee! Murderous monster! cried Manfred—can assassins forgive? I took thee for Isabella; but heaven directed my bloody hand to the heart of my child!—Oh! Matilda—I cannot utter it—canst thou forgive the blindness of my rage?—I can, I do, and may heaven confirm it! said Matilda—But while I have life to ask it—oh, my mother! what will she feel!—Will you comfort her, my lord? Will you not put her away? Indeed she loves you—Oh, I am faint! bear me to the castle—can I live to have her close my eyes?

Theodore and the monks besought her earnestly to suffer herself to be borne into the convent; but her instances were so pressing to be carried to the castle, that, placing her on a litter, they conveyed her thither as she requested. Theodore supporting her head with his arm, and hanging over her in an agony of despairing love, still endeavoured to inspire her with hopes of life. Jerome on the other side comforted her with discourses of heaven, and holding a crucifix before her, which she bathed with innocent tears, prepared her for her passage to immortality. Manfred, plunged in the deepest affliction, followed the litter in despair.

Ere they reached the castle, Hippolita, informed of the dreadful catastrophe, had flown to meet her murdered child; but when she saw the afflicted procession, the mightiness of her grief deprived her of her senses, and she fell lifeless to the earth in a swoon. Isabella and Frederic, who attended her, were overwhelmed in almost equal sorrow. Matilda alone seemed insensible to her own situation: every thought was lost in tenderness for her mother. Ordering the litter to stop, as soon as Hippolita was brought to herself, she asked for her father. He approached, unable to speak. Matilda, seizing his hand and her mother's, locked them in her own, and then clasped them to her heart. Manfred could not support this act of pathetic piety. He dashed himself on the ground, and cursed the day he was born. Isabella, apprehensive that these struggles of passion were more than Matilda could support, took upon herself to order Manfred to be borne to his apartment, while she caused Matilda to be conveyed to the nearest chamber. Hippolita, scarce more alive than her daughter, was regardless of every thing but her: but when the tender Isabella's care would have likewise removed her, while the surgeons examined Matilda's wound, she cried, Remove me? Never! never! I lived but in her, and will expire with her. Matilda raised her eyes at her mother's voice, but closed them again without speaking. Her sinking pulse, and the damp coldness of her hand, soon dispelled all hopes of recovery. Theodore followed the surgeons into the outer chamber, and heard them pronounce the fatal sentence with a transport equal to phrensy—Since she cannot live mine, cried he, at least she shall be mine in death!—Father! Jerome! will you not join our hands? cried he to the friar, who with the marquis had accompanied the surgeons. What means thy distracted rashness? said Jerome: is this an hour for marriage? It is, it is, cried Theodore: alas, there is no other! Young man, thou art too unadvised, said Frederic: dost thou think we are to listen to thy fond transports in this hour of fate? What pretensions hast thou to the princess? Those of a prince, said Theodore; of the sovereign of Otranto. This reverend man, my father, has informed me who I am. Thou ravest, said the marquis: there is no prince of Otranto but myself now Manfred by murder, by sacrilegious murder, has forfeited all pretensions. My lord, said Jerome, assuming an air of command, he tells you true. It was not my purpose the secret should have been divulged so soon; but fate presses onward to its work. What his hotheaded passion has revealed, my tongue confirms. Know, prince, that when Alfonso set sail for the Holy Land— Is this a season for explanations? cried Theodore. Father, come and unite me to the princess: she shall be mine—in every other thing I will dutifully obey you. My life! my adored Matilda! continued Theodore, rushing back into the inner chamber, will you not be mine? will you not bless your——Isabella made signs to him to be silent, apprehending the princess was near her end. What, is she dead? cried Theodore: is it possible? The violence of his exclamations brought Matilda to herself. Lifting up her eyes she looked round for her mother—Life of my soul! I am here, cried Hippolita: think not I will quit thee!—Oh! you are too good, said Matilda—but weep not for me, my mother! I am going where sorrow never dwells.—Isabella, thou hast loved me; wot thou not supply my fondness to this dear, dear woman? Indeed I am faint!—Oh! my child! my child! said Hippolita in a flood of tears, can I not withhold thee a moment?—It will not be, said Matilda—Commend me to heaven—Where is my father? Forgive him, dearest mother—forgive him my death; it was an error—Oh! I had forgotten—Dearest mother, I vowed never to see Theodore more—Perhaps that has drawn down this calamity—but it was not intentional—can you pardon me?—Oh! wound not my agonizing soul! said Hippolita; thou never couldst offend me.—Alas, she faints! Help! help!—I would say something more, said Matilda struggling, but it wonnot* be—Isabella—Theodore—for my sake—oh!—She expired. Isabella and her women tore Hippolita from the corse; but Theodore threatened destruction to all who attempted to remove him from it. He printed a thousand kisses on her clay-cold hands, and uttered every expression that despairing love could dictate.

Isabella, in the mean time, was accompanying the afflicted Hippolita to her apartment; but in the middle of the court they were met by Manfred, who, distracted with his own thoughts, and anxious once more to behold his daughter, was advancing to the chamber where she lay. As the moon was now at its height, he read in the countenances of this unhappy company the event he dreaded. What! is she dead? cried he in wild confusion—A clap of thunder at that instant shook the castle to its foundations; the earth rocked, and the clank of more than mortal armour was heard behind. Frederic and Jerome thought the last day was at hand. The latter, forcing Theodore along with them, rushed into the court. The moment Theodore appeared, the walls of the castle behind Manfred were thrown down with a mighty force, and the form of Alfonso, dilated to an immense magnitude, appeared in the centre of the ruins. Behold in Theodore, the true heir of Alfonso! said the vision: and having pronounced those words, accompanied by a clap of thunder, it ascended solemnly towards heaven, where the clouds parting asunder, the form of saint Nicholas was seen; and receiving Alfonso's shade, they were soon wrapt from mortal eyes in a blaze of glory.

The beholders fell prostrate on their faces, acknowledging the divine will. The first that broke silence was Hippolita. My lord, said she to the desponding Manfred, behold the vanity of human greatness! Conrad is gone! Matilda is no more! in Theodore we view the true prince of Otranto. By what miracle he is so, I know not—suffice it to us, our doom is pronounced! Shall we not, can we but dedicate the few deplorable hours we have to live, in deprecating the farther wrath of heaven? Heaven ejects us—whither can we fly, but to yon holy cells that yet offer us a retreat?—Thou guiltless but unhappy woman! unhappy by my crimes! replied Manfred, my heart at last is open to thy devout admonitions. Oh! could—but it cannot be—ye are lost in wonder—let me at last do justice on myself! To heap shame on my own head is all the satisfaction I have left to offer to offended heaven. My story has drawn down these judgments: let my confession atone—But ah! what can atone for usurpation and a murdered child? a child murdered in a consecrated place!——List, sirs, and may this bloody record be a warning to future tyrants!

Alfonso, ye all know, died in the Holy Land—Ye would interrupt me; ye would say he came not fairly to his end—It is most true—why else this bitter cup which Manfred must drink to the dregs? Ricardo, my grandfather, was his chamberlain—I would draw a veil over my ancestor's crimes—but it is in vain: Alfonso died by poison. A fictitious will declared Ricardo his heir. His crimes pursued him—yet he lost no Conrad, no Matilda! I pay the price of usurpation for all! A storm overtook him. Haunted by his guilt, he vowed to saint Nicholas to found a church and two convents if he lived to reach Otranto. The sacrifice was accepted: the saint appeared to him in a dream, and promised that Ricardo's posterity should reign in Otranto until the rightful owner should be grown too large to inhabit the castle, and as long as issue-male from Ricardo's loins should remain to enjoy it.—Alas! alas! nor male nor female, except myself, remains of all his wretched race!—I have done—the woes of these three days speak the rest. How this young man can be Alfonso's heir I know not—yet I do not doubt it. His are these dominions; I resign them—yet I knew not Alfonso had an heir—I question not the will of heaven— poverty and prayer must fill up the woeful space, until Manfred shall be summoned to Ricardo.

What remains is my part to declare, said Jerome. When Alfonso set sail for the Holy Land, he was driven by a storm on the coast of Sicily. The other vessel, which bore Ricardo and his train, as your *lordship* must have heard, was separated from him. It is most true, said Manfred; and the title you give me is more than an out-cast can claim—Well, be it so—proceed. Jerome blushed, and continued. For three months lord Alfonso was wind-bound in Sicily. There he became enamoured of a fair virgin named Victoria. He was too pious to tempt her to forbidden pleasures. They were married. Yet deeming this amour incongruous with the holy vow of arms by which he was bound, he was determined to conceal their nuptials until his return from the crusado, when he purposed to seek and acknowledge her for his lawful wife. He left her pregnant. During his absence she was delivered of a daughter: but scarce had she felt a mother's pangs, ere she heard the fatal rumour of her lord's death, and the succession of Ricardo. What could a friendless, helpless woman do? would her testimony avail?—Yet, my lord, I have an authentic writing.—It needs not, said Manfred; the horrors of these days, the vision we have but now seen, all corroborate thy evidence beyond a thousand parchments. Matilda's death and my expulsion—Be com-

posed, my lord, said Hippolita; this holy man did not mean
to recall your griefs. Jerome proceeded.

I shall not dwell on what is needless. The daughter of
which Victoria was delivered, was at her maturity bestowed
in marriage on me. Victoria died; and the secret remained
locked in my breast. Theodore's narrative has told the rest.

The friar ceased. The disconsolate company retired to the
remaining part of the castle. In the morning Manfred signed
his abdication of the principality, with the approbation of
Hippolita, and each took on them the habit of religion in the
neighbouring convents. Frederic offered his daughter to the
new prince, which Hippolita's tenderness for Isabella concurred to promote: but Theodore's grief was too fresh to
admit the thought of another love; and it was not till after
frequent discourses with Isabella, of his dear Matilda, that
he was persuaded he could know no happiness but in the
society of one with whom he could forever indulge the
melancholy that had taken possession of his soul.

# EXPLANATORY NOTES

3 *Epigraph*: added to the title-page of the second edition. This is an adaptation of lines 7–9 of Horace's *Ars Poetica*: *'vanae | fingentur species, ut nec pes nec caput uni | reddatur formae'* ('idle fancies shall be shaped [like a sick man's dream] so that neither foot nor head can be assigned to a single shape'). As W. S. Lewis has observed, Walpole reverses the meaning to say that 'nevertheless head and foot are assigned to a single shape', with interesting implications. *Ars Poetica* was the *locus classicus* of the neo-classical rule of probability, and the lines, in their original context relate to the proper reception of grotesque images: laughter and mockery. Walpole's alteration makes reference to the plot of his novel (the dismembered limbs of the spectre Alfonso are eventually put back in order), and also suggests that although the elements of *The Castle of Otranto* may violate the laws of nature, they nevertheless form an imaginative unity.

5 *black letter*: gothic type used by the early printers, as distinguished from the roman face now in use.

*purest Italian*: Walpole set the trend for locating 'Gothic' fiction in Italy, rather than in the northern parts of Europe native to the Goths. In the eighteenth century, Italy was the Mecca of classical culture, the highlight of the Grand Tour of the Continent made by many young gentlemen (including Walpole) in order to complete their education. The frequent use of southern European settings in Gothic fiction is generally attributed to a mixture of Protestant prejudice and a stereotyped notion of strong Mediterranean passions.

*not long afterwards*: Walpole's tale has some features in common with the history of the Hohenstaufen dynasty, rulers of the Kingdom of Sicily (including the southern part of the peninsula, where Otranto is located). Frederick II, Holy Roman Emperor and leader of the fifth Crusade (1228–9), was locked in rivalry with the papacy over the control of Italy until his death in 1250; for many years it was believed by his supporters that he would one day return. His successor Conrad was stranded in Germany, and Frederick's illegitimate son, Manfred of Taranto, became viceroy in the Southern Italian kingdom, defeating the papal army at Foggia in 1254. Conrad died on his way through Italy, and his heir, the infant Conradin, remained in Germany. In 1258 Manfred exploited rumours of the death of the child to declare himself King. The Pope, determined to eradicate the Staufen line, persuaded Charles of Anjou to oppose the usurper, and in 1266 Manfred was defeated and killed at the battle of Benevento. Unlike his fictional namesake, King Manfred, with his wife Helena, had four sons, who were kept in chains by the conqueror until they died.

5 *Arragonian kings in Naples*: Peter III of Aragon, King of Spain, had laid claim to Southern Italy in 1282 by virtue of his marriage to a daughter of King Manfred. He took the island of Sicily, but the establishment of Aragon in Naples did not come until Alfonso V captured the city in 1442. Spanish rule, interrupted by various contests and conflicts, continued into the eighteenth century.

6 *rules of the drama*: a reference to 'the three unities' of neo-classical dramatic theory, intended to enhance verisimilitude. They are 'unity of action', whereby the parts of a narrative are 'so closely connected that the transposal or withdrawal of any one of them will disjoint and dislocate the whole' (Aristotle, *Poetics*, sect. 8); 'unity of place', restricting the action to a single location; and 'unity of time', ideally limiting the duration of the represented action to the length of the performance, or at most to twenty-four hours.

7 *saint Nicholas*: the reason for the prominence of St Nicholas in the story is uncertain, although the remains of Nicholas of Myra, a bishop of the fourth century, are kept at Bari, not far from Otranto, and there are many legends of his power as a miracle-worker.

8 *some real castle*: the principal model is Strawberry Hill, but Walpole was later struck by the similarity between one of the colleges at Cambridge University (probably Trinity) and his mental image of the castle. In 1786 he was delighted to discover that there really was a castle at Otranto, when a friend made him the gift of a sketch of it; he had chosen the name from a map of Naples simply because it was 'well-sounding'. See W. S. Lewis, 'The Genesis of Strawberry Hill', *Metropolitan Museum Studies*, 5: 1 (June 1934), 88–90, and Warren Hunting Smith, 'Strawberry Hill and Otranto', *Times Literary Supplement*, 23 May 1936, 440.

9 *two kinds of romance, the ancient and the modern*: see Introduction, pp. xii–xiii.

*powers of fancy*: see Introduction, pp. xiii–xiv.

*rules of probability*: the first criterion of neo-classical criticism is that the spectator or reader must believe in a fiction in order to be moved or delighted and, ultimately, instructed by it. The rule applies to action, characterization, and diction. See also note to p. 4.

11 *That great master of nature, Shakespeare, was the model I copied*: see introduction, pp. xiv–xv.

*omitted, or vested in heroics*: it was common practice on the London stage of the time to perform Shakespeare's tragedies in versions which excluded or altered such scenes in keeping with neo-classical taste.

*Voltaire*: the pen-name of François-Marie Arouet (1694–1778), a leading figure of the Enlightenment. From 1726 to 1729, he lived in exile in England. After his return to France, he became an influential disseminator of English culture, publishing commentaries on the work of Shakespeare and other poets and playwrights, as well as Newton and Locke, all at that time almost unknown in the rest of Europe. In his view, Shakespeare was a primitive, capable of poetry of surpassing genius, but lacking the art of the great French dramatists of the seventeenth century, Corneille and Racine. This opinion of their relative merits is reiterated in his edition of the collected works of Corneille, *Le Théâtre de Pierre Corneille avec des commentaires*, published in twelve volumes in 1763. The complaint that there is 'scarcely a tragedy by Shakespeare where one doesn't find the jokes of coarse men side by side with the sublimity of heroes' appears in the preface to *Le Cid*, in *The Complete Works of Voltaire*, ed. Theodore Besterman *et al.* (Geneva and Banbury, 1968–   ), liv. 38–9.

*twice translated the same speech in Hamlet . . . latterly in derision*: the famous soliloquy from *Hamlet* beginning 'To be or not to be', translated first in *Lettres philosophiques*, originally published in English as *Letters Concerning the English Nation* (1733), in letter XVIII 'On Tragedy'; secondly in *Appel à toutes les nations de l'Europe* (1761). Both the translations, with commentary, are reproduced in Theodore Besterman (ed.), *Studies on Voltaire and the Eighteenth Century*, liv. *Voltaire on Shakespeare* (Geneva, 1967).

11 *the same person*: see Voltaire's preface to *Le Comte d'Essex*, in *Commentaires sur Corneille, Complete Works*, lv. 1002.

12 *On y voit un melange . . . le mieux traité*: 'We find there a mixture of seriousness and jesting, of the comic and the pathetic; often even a single incident produces all these contrasts. Nothing is more common than a house in which a father is scolding, a daughter—absorbed in her emotions—weeping; the son makes fun of both of them, some relatives take different sides in the scene, etc. We do not infer from this that every comedy ought to have scenes of buffoonery and scenes of touching emotion: there are many very good plays in which gaiety alone reigns; others entirely serious; others mixed; others where compassion gives rise to tears: no genre should be ruled out: and if someone were to ask me which genre is best, I would reply, the one which is best handled.' From 'Préface de l'éditeur de l'édition de 1738' of Voltaire's play *Mérope* (1736); *Œuvres Complètes de Voltaire*, ed. Louis Moland, new edition (Paris, 1883), iii. 443. The preface to *L'Enfant prodigue* was written by Voltaire himself, as Walpole suspected.

12 *Maffei*: Scipione, Count (1675–1755), an Italian scholar whose tragic drama *Mérope* (1713) was a great success and rapidly went through many editions. Voltaire wrote his own play on the subject and prefaced it with a letter to Maffei reflecting on differences in dramatic practice among European nations.

13 *Tous ces traits . . . espece* [sic] *de simplicité*: 'All these features are naïve: all are appropriate to the people you bring on stage, and the manners you give them. These natural familiarities would have been, I believe, well received in Athens; but Paris and our audience demand a different kind of simplicity.' From 'A M. Le Marquis Scipio Maffei' prefixed to *Mérope* (1743); *Œuvres Complètes*, iv. 188.

*a discussion of the espece* [sic] *de simplicité*: Walpole quotes Voltaire, from the letter to Maffei, but implies the derogatory sense of *simplicité*, 'silliness'.

*parterre*: literally, the area occupied by standing spectators in front of the stage; figuratively, the most discerning section of the audience.

*difficiles nugæ*: laboured trivialities; Martial, *Epigrams* ii. 86. 9.

14 *singled out to defend in Racine*: See '[Remarques sur] Bérénice, tragédie', in *Commentaires sur Corneille, Complete Works*, lv. 941.

*ichnography*: the ground-plan.

*a second time*: refers to Voltaire's initial enthusiasm for *Hamlet*, noted on p. 11.

*whatever rank their suffrages allot to it*: Walpole plays on the idea of a 'republic of letters', with a populist twist. It is suggested that however the critics—the officially 'enfranchised' members of the public—rate the book, the general public has already ensured its success.

15 *Lady Mary Coke*: the sonnet was added to the second edition. Lady Mary Coke (1726–1811), was a friend of Walpole, and a prominent and eccentric figure in Court circles.

17 *A Gothic Story*: see Introduction, pp. x, xv.

21 *poignarded*: stabbed with a dagger or poignard.

26 *the portrait of his grandfather . . . uttered a deep sigh and heaved its breast*: Walpole identified a portrait in his own possession, 'of Lord Falkland all in white' by Paul van Somer (1576–1621), as the model (*Walpole's Correspondence*, 1. 88; letter to William Cole, 9 Mar. 1763). The reviewer of *Otranto* in the *Critical Review* (19 Jan. 1765, 50–1), took particular note of the portrait as grounds for doubting the antiquity of the story: 'We cannot help thinking that this circumstance is some presumption that the castle of Otranto is a modern fabrick; for we doubt much whether pictures were fastened in pannels before the year 1243.' In Scott's Introduction to the novel he cites another reviewer (from the *Quarterly Review*, Oct. 1817) who proposes that an incident from *The Jerusalem* by the Spanish dramatist Lope de Vega (1562–1635), may have been Walpole's inspiration.

*Lead on! cried Manfred; I will follow thee to the gulph of perdition*: cf. Hamlet's address to the ghost of his father, 'Go on, I'll follow thee!' (1. iv. 63) and Horatio's caution, 'What if it tempt you toward the flood, my lord, | Or to the dreadful summit of the cliff' (1. iv. 50–1). The ghost scenes from *Hamlet* are a direct inspiration for several passages of the novel.

27 *a subterraneous passage*: see Introduction, p. xvi.

30 *essay*: trial.

31 *disculpate*: clear from blame.

31 *Peace! blockhead*: the exchange recalls the tyrant Macbeth's insulting treatment of messengers in *Macbeth*, v. ii and v.

34 *comprehensive*: for 'apprehensive'; a malapropism.

35 *I saw his foot and part of his leg*: Anna Laetitia Barbauld (née Aikin) identifies a tale of the fantastic by Anthony Hamilton, 'Le Bélier' (1730), as a source for the giant limbs (introduction to *The Castle of Otranto*, in Barbauld (ed.), *The British Novelists* (London, 1810), xii, p. ii). Giganticism was also a common feature of oriental tales, which were very popular in the period.

38 *pallet-bed*: a bed with a straw mattress, or simply a small or humble bed.

41 *orisons*: prayers (arch.).

42 *If they are spirits in pain, we may ease their sufferings by questioning them*: see Horatio's address to the ghost of King Hamlet: 'If there be any good thing to be done | That may to thee do ease and grace to me, | Speak to me' (*Hamlet*, i. i. 111–13).

43 *sift*: question.

44 *Speak quickly, said Matilda; the morning dawns apace*: cf. *Romeo and Juliet*, iii. v. 35.

45 *spark*: one who affect smartness or display in dress or manners.

46 *postern-gate*: a back or private gate.

   *another-guess mould*: another sort of nature.

47 *good-liking*: approval.

48 *[Manfred's colour changed]*: an unusual use of square brackets, as if for stage directions. This tale is compared to a drama by Walpole in the first Preface, and by Warburton; see Introduction, p. xx.

49 *Cant*: to use pious language as a matter of form.

51 *related to me in the fourth degree*: a measure of consanguinity in relationship, the degree determined by the number of steps up on the genealogical chart to a common ancestor and downward to the relative in question. Civil law counted all the steps and canon law counted only the steps from the common ancestor to the party in question: thus an uncle and niece would be related in the third degree according to civil and in the second degree according to canon law. Whichever system

is being used, Manfred's later claim that he and Hippolita are related 'within the forbidden degrees' (p. 69) seems rather far-fetched, and it is not surprising that here he adds a quibble over a prior marriage-contract.

52 *fulminated*: literally, thundered. The Catholic Church fulminated by striking with its 'thunderbolts' of ecclesiastical censure.

*traverse his views*: obstruct his plans.

54 *boarded*: panelled.

57 *discovered the mark of a bloody arrow*: the discovery of parentage and noble birth is one of the most typical conventions of romance. Usually it prepares the way for a happy ending by eliminating disparities in the rank of two lovers, and at the same time resolves ideological tensions in the narrative by reinforcing the conservative view that status and inner merit are linked, and that gentility will shine through in spite of circumstances. Walpole employs the device with an ironic twist, since the rise of Theodore up the social scale entails the demotion of his beloved, Matilda, and contributes to the final tragedy.

58 *brazen*: brass.

61 *warder*: a staff, wand, or baton carried as a symbol of authority; here used to signal a challenge.

63 *management*: diplomacy.

64 *the holy princess Sanchia of Arragon*: probably Walpole has confused the daughter of Sancho of Aragon (in the eleventh century) and the daughter of Sancho I of Portugal (in the thirteenth). St Sancia of Portugal (d. 1229) founded a convent at Cellas and took the veil herself there. Her brother had at one time urged her to marry her nephew in order to make peace between Spain and Portugal.

*the cavalcade arrived*: W. S. Lewis has proposed that for this scene Walpole drew on Segar's *Honour, Military and Civil* (1602) and Morgan's *Sphere of Gentry* (1661), as part of his aim of presenting an accurate picture of medieval chivalry. Scott praises this attention to 'the costume of the period' in his introduction (*Lives of the Novelists*, London [1910], 197).

*harbingers*: attendants who announce an arrival.

65 *quarterly*: that is, on a shield divided into four parts by vertical and horizontal lines, the arms of Vicenza were placed in

one diagonal pair and those of Otranto in the other. Manfred is offended by the implicit claim to his title.

65 *beavers*: the lower part of the face-guard of a helmet, when worn with a visor, but sometimes serving the purposes of both.

*cartel*: the written challenge.

66 *gage*: pledge.

*hospital*: hostel for the reception of knights.

68 *vitious*: unlawful.

74 *the effect of pent-up vapours*: this risible explanation looks forward to the technique of the 'explained supernatural', whereby apparently supernatural phenomena, having served their purpose in creating terror and suspense, are reduced in the end to natural causes. Ann Radcliffe was its principal practitioner; Scott condemned her 'attempt to reconcile the superstitious credulity of feudal ages with the philosophic scepticism of our own', preferring Walpole's 'bold assertion of the actual existence of phantoms and apparitions' as more in keeping 'with the manners of ancient times' (*Lives of the Novelists*, 200).

75 *the caves*: in this brief episode Walpole manages to draw on the multiple symbolism of caves. In the romance genre, caves feature as a refuge from persecution; Shakespeare's *Cymbeline* is a notable example. The melancholic recourse to caves and forests is another tradition dating from the Renaissance period. In the eighteenth century caves and grottoes, natural and artificial, became a popular feature of garden design, and 'hermits' were sometimes hired to inhabit them and enhance the Gothic effect. The mysterious darkness of the cave can be seen as a figure for the allure of fictional terrors.

*approve*: demonstrate.

76 *what would a censorious world think of my conduct?*: Isabella's concern with propriety at a moment of peril has sometimes been taken as a comic touch. However, similar episodes appear in all seriousness in the work of Ann Radcliffe, most famously in *Mysteries of Udolpho* when Emily, fleeing for her life from an Apennine fortress, becomes aware that she has forgotten her hat, and in *The Italian*, where Ellena hesitates before agreeing to be saved by her lover from imprisonment in a convent. Although it is hard for modern readers to credit this degree of nicety over decorum, an

eighteenth-century audience may well have relished the drama of a choice between physical oppression on the one hand, and on the other, social rejection, the 'fate worse than death' which would follow loss of reputation.

80 *Joppa*: now Jaffa, a port in Israel.

82 *glosing*: the act of explaining away or extenuating.

83 *Why do you fix your eye-balls thus?*: the episode is strongly reminiscent of the banquet scene in *Macbeth*, where Lady Macbeth asks Macbeth, terror-struck by the apparition of the murdered Banquo, 'Why do you make such faces?' (III. iv. 66), but it also recalls the scenes from *Hamlet* in which the ghost of the King is recognized by the armour he wears.

84 *taken by corsairs from the coast of Sicily*: abduction by pirates was a favoured device of romances from the ancient Greeks onwards, but Walpole is also historically accurate. Muslim pirates periodically terrorized coastal areas of Italy in the medieval era. In the eighteenth century, travel by boat on the Mediterranean was still considered a perilous enterprise.

94 *Will heaven visit the innocent for the crimes of the guilty?*: the injustice of divine providence is suggested here, and on pp. 113–14. See Introduction, p. xxxi.

97 *lance her anathema*: hurl a curse of excommunication and of damnation.

*three drops of blood fell from the nose of Alfonso's statue*: a slightly ludicrous variation on a standard type of Catholic miracle, perhaps indicating Walpole's sceptical purpose. But blood, in the form of stains, trickles, pools, or inundations, was to become the staple of the horror mode.

98 *they wither away like the grass, and their place knows them no more*: biblical resonances: Isaiah 40: 6; 1 Peter 1: 24; Job 7: 6.

99 *his reliance on ancient prophecies*: comparable to Macbeth's false reliance on the Witches' prophecies.

100 *oriel window*: a recess projecting from the outside wall, supported by brackets.

*vulnerary herbs*: herbs with healing properties.

101 *by my halidame*: a common oath down to the sixteenth century; a 'halidame' or 'halidome' is a holy relic or any object regarded as sacred.

*though I am poor, I am honest*: proverbial.

103 *watchet-coloured chamber*: light blue or sky-blue. There was a Blue Bedchamber at Strawberry Hill.

106 *advertised*: informed.

*Angels of grace, protect me!*: cf. *Hamlet*, I. iv. 20: 'Angels and ministers of grace, defend us!'

112 *wonnot*: elided form of 'will not'.

*The*
*Oxford*
*World's*
*Classics*
*Website*

**www.worldsclassics.co.uk**

- Information about new titles
- Explore the full range of Oxford World's Classics
- Links to other literary sites and the main OUP webpage
- Imaginative competitions, with bookish prizes
- Peruse the Oxford World's Classics Magazine
- Articles by editors
- Extracts from Introductions
- A forum for discussion and feedback on the series
- Special information for teachers and lecturers

**www.worldsclassics.co.uk**

**American Literature**

**British and Irish Literature**

**Children's Literature**

**Classics and Ancient Literature**

**Colonial Literature**

**Eastern Literature**

**European Literature**

**History**

**Medieval Literature**

**Oxford English Drama**

**Poetry**

**Philosophy**

**Politics**

**Religion**

**The Oxford Shakespeare**

A complete list of Oxford Paperbacks, including Oxford World's Classics, Oxford Shakespeare, Oxford Drama, and Oxford Paperback Reference, is available in the UK from the Academic Division Publicity Department, Oxford University Press, Great Clarendon Street, Oxford OX2 6DP.

In the USA, complete lists are available from the Paperbacks Marketing Manager, Oxford University Press, 198 Madison Avenue, New York, NY 10016.

Oxford Paperbacks are available from all good bookshops. In case of difficulty, customers in the UK can order direct from Oxford University Press Bookshop, Freepost, 116 High Street, Oxford OX1 4BR, enclosing full payment. Please add 10 per cent of published price for postage and packing.